KU-454-198

The Missing Workforce

Managing Absenteeism

Andrew Sargent

Institute of Personnel Management

First published 1989
© Andrew Sargent 1989

All rights reserved. No part of this publication may
be reproduced, stored in a retrieval system, or
transmitted in any form or by any means, electronic,
mechanical, photocopying, recording or otherwise,
without written permission of the Institute of
Personnel Management, IPM House, Camp Road,
Wimbledon, London SW19 4UX.

Phototypeset by Input Typesetting Ltd, London
and printed in Great Britain by
Dotesios Printers Ltd., Trowbridge, Wiltshire

British Library Cataloguing in Publication Data
Sargent, Andrew,
    The missing workforce.
    1. Personnel. Absenteeism. Management aspects
    I. Title   II. Institute of Personnel Management
    658.3'14

ISBN 0–85292–411–9

WITHDRAWN

The Missing Workforce

Managing Absenteeism

1995

ι

ι A

ι A

LIVERPOOL POLYTECHNIC LIBRARY

3 1111 00423 1450

Sargent, A
The missing workforce: managing absentee
P M 658.314 SAR 1989

WITHDRAWN

Contents

*To Amanda Jane
and Caroline Jenny*

Author's Note

Some two years ago I produced with Guild Sound and Vision a film about managing attendance entitled *Gone Today – Here Tommow*, which formed part of a complete training package. Accompanying it were two small booklets, which I wrote. I mention them here only because I have had to take them into account in writing this book for IPM. Since it is difficult to write the same book twice, I've updated and enlarged my previous efforts, but incorporated material from them in this volume. I therefore acknowledge Guild Sound and Vision's film and publications department for allowing me to adapt such material in this way.

This book is based almost entirely on my own personal experience and observation and on the sound practice of good employers. Since 1971 I've worked as a consultant in a wide variety of different industries, including

The Civil Service
Commerce
Data processing
Construction
Local authorities
The National Health Service
Manufacturing
Retailing
Distribution
Docks and dockyards
Quarrying
Oil
Print and publishing
Public relations.

Wherever I've been I've never found people any different.

Acknowledgements

I should like to acknowledge the help of a number of colleagues and friends:

Rhiannon Green, who, with enormous patience, kept re-reading the manuscript and contributing to it

Yvonne Bennion, who is always an unending source of information and advice

Pat Lennon, whose clarity of mind must be an asset to any organization

Graham Robinson, for allowing me to edit and alter Tesco's Absence Policy

Daphne Smith, for typing the original manuscript.

I should also acknowledge everything I learnt earlier in my career from John Garnett, latterly of the Industrial Society. I won't acknowledge the firms that provided the examples. This is for obvious reasons. However, they know who they are.

Introduction

Dear Personnel Manager,

This is a book about managing attendance and it won't be helpful unless we define right now what 'attendance' and 'absenteeism' mean. So, as a preamble to the rest of this book, consider these simple guidance principles which might help prevent you from cracking a nut with a sledgehammer.

'Attendance' is a positive expression – and 'absenteeism' is negative. The object of the exercise is to get people to come to work, not simply to deal with the absentees.

Two or three days off a year is not a problem. Certainly we should see every employee every time they're away. But that's just to find out what was wrong and make sure they know we care – and that we missed them.

Two or three days a month (or even every two months) *is* a problem. Two days a month means an absence rate in excess of 10%, i.e. the attendance figure is only 90% when it ought to be around 98%.

The hints in this book are intended to help you deal with people who are in the one or two days a month bracket – or worse. They may not look like a problem but they are.

If you have absentees who are above this level in their time off, this book will still help – but you should beware. You may be dealing with a professional, someone who knows the system better than you. You might need more specialist help, e.g. from a lawyer.

If you have long-term absence problems then this book may still be relevant. But if you're looking for detailed assistance on what to do about the chronically sick employee, you should look elsewhere.

If you want professional guidance on absence and the law, you will probably be better off talking to an industrial lawyer. I'm not a lawyer. I'm in the business of passing on commonsense and experience.

As you read this book you'll notice it says a lot about motivation and about the role of line managers in providing it. I make no apologies! That's where I am on the subject. Motivating employees isn't a personnel manager's job – it's the job of the person accountable for performance. And absenteeism is a measure of performance.

If you don't agree with that, that's your right. But don't think I'm suggesting personnel has no role in managing motivation and controlling absence. Far from it. I believe personnel specialists are crucial: as facilitators, coaches and counsellors, but not as providers of instant solutions.

Finally, this is, I hope, a practical book which provides useful assistance in the areas described in these guidelines. What I've done is:

define the problem
explain why it is a problem
examine what causes it
examine the part personnel should play
define the job of line management
discuss the role of unions
set out some hints on training.

These areas are my experience. Where I'm not experienced in a subject, I haven't written about it. There are a lot of examples. They're all true. They all happened either to me or to people I know.

I hope you find it all useful.

Andrew Sargent

Chapter 1
The British Disease

Absenteeism is one of the recurrent British diseases. The fact is that it has been going on for years and there is nothing new about it at all. Since time immemorial, working people at every level have considered it their right to take a day off from time to time. It doesn't mean that everybody is inherently lazy or that Britain is a nation beset by chronic illness or influenza. What it does mean, however, is that the habit of 'going sick' occasionally has become ingrained into the subconscious of millions of working men and women. This is not to say it's an acceptable behaviour pattern. Only that it happens.

A great deal of statistical evidence supports this contention. Surveys carried out by the Industrial Society and the CBI and other bodies have discovered that the national average absence rate varies between 4½% and 6%, depending upon the part of the country in which the enquiries are conducted. This may not sound a great deal until you work out that between 4½% and 6% actually means between 1½ and 2½ weeks per year. That is to say that the average working person is away for an extra two weeks on top of his or her annual holiday entitlement. That, by anybody's definition, is a great deal of time.

This is not a book about how to manage the problem of chronic illness. On the contrary, it is a book about how to manage absenteeism of a far more casual kind – minor discomfort, problems away from work and maybe 'pulling a fast one'. If your problem is what to do with the chronically sick, the person who, because of some physical condition or other, has not been able to come to work for six months or a year, you should also consult a doctor or your company lawyer. Both of them are in a far better position to give you practical advice. If, however, your problem is with that rather more subtle form of absenteeism, the odd day off – taken by literally hundreds of thousands of employees each year – then read on!

The cost is enormous. It is so enormous that official figures are hard to establish and verify. But it is an intrinsically important part of the argument and we shall return to it later on, under the heading 'The Extent of the Problem' and in Chapter 3. For the time being, let's just say that if all those who had jobs actually turned up for them, Britain would be a *far* more prosperous place than it actually is.

This is not to suggest that we should return to those dark days when absence itself was punishable by the industrial sledgehammer of dismissal. On the contrary, most people recognize that we have reached the age of prosperity. We have actually achieved the first part of the Marxist doctrine which says words to the effect of 'unto each according to his needs'. Our problem is much more subtle. What we're now looking for is the achievement of the second part: 'and from each according to his ability'. In many ways, absentee problems encapsulate that particular challenge.

It goes without saying that from time to time people, for various reasons, are going to be unable to go to work. Many would rightly argue that this is a desirable state of affairs. Who wants to punish 'flu victims? Who wants to victimize people who have normal discomforts with which they would be far better off spending a morning in bed? Who wants to destroy the career of the young employee who occasionally slips over on one of life's banana skins and for self-inflicted reasons is too ill to go to work on Monday morning?

But, at the same time, what employer wants to put up with the habitual absence from work of the old stager who knows perfectly well that, if he does not bother to come in every third or fourth Monday, nobody is actually going to do anything about it? Why should managers tolerate professional 'lead swinging'? And yet for some reason they do. Many companies seem almost happy to live with a situation in which 5% (or maybe more) of their employees are away on any particular working day. It is an odd state of affairs but it's one which is allowed by thousands of companies – and millions of managers – to continue.

To plagiarize Shakespeare: some people are born lazy – and some become lazy later on! But not all absence is about laziness; to assume that would be almost as big a mistake as assuming laziness has nothing to do with it.

Of course, there are *some* people who can't get out of bed in the morning, and the fact that they can't, and are allowed to get away with it, has an undeniable influence on their colleagues. A few, maybe more, inevitably follow suit and later on still others sometimes feel they have no alternative other than to copy them.

In one leading British manufacturer it is common knowledge that everybody is expected to take a standard amount of 'time off'. Sometimes it is called 'your rights'. What is meant by the expression is that a certain number of days off are allowed in the company's sickness procedure for which people need not complete any self-certification or provide any medical evidence for their absence from work. It has become commonly understood that such days will be given without unreasonable argument and the result is that a number of employees habitually take them. At counselling interviews some people claim that they are virtually expected to do so! I can remember, in one of my early jobs, being effectively told to do it!

But, as I have said, absenteeism is not simply about laziness. There are an enormous number of reasons why people sometimes can't go to work. They include domestic problems, family difficulties, emotional issues and a whole host of environmental factors which in their way conspire to make it easier to stay at home rather than turn up. What all these factors have in common, however, is that they can in some way be *managed*, provided that the employee concerned receives some help. Personnel specialists can do a great deal to ensure that this kind of help is offered. It is all a question of knowing employees well enough to be able to predict their behaviour, and that means working closely with managers and helping them find out exactly what makes their people 'tick'.

Ninety per cent of the time, the problem is about relationships. Employees often don't feel that they know their managers well enough to be able to explain that the child minder can't come in, that one of the children is sick, that the elderly mother who lives with them has fallen out of bed and needs constant nursing attention. Certainly they often feel they can't explain their own personal or perhaps physical difficulties. Rather than talk about them, individuals stay away. The consequence is that everybody suffers, and that includes the firm.

Communications play an enormously important part in absence control, and the company that doesn't train its managers and supervisors and consistently coach them in how to relate to people, listen to people and counsel them omits to do so at its peril.

This is especially true today, since we live in an era from which both the stick and the carrot have effectively been removed. Once upon a time it was possible to threaten people who did not conform with dismissal. The introduction of employment-protection legislation has effectively cut out such a negative approach to management. Yet, at the same time, it is no longer possible simply to bribe people to come to work, because (life being what it is) they are now subtle enough to simply say: 'Well, I will take the money, but that doesn't guarantee I will conform to the standards that you, the company, require.'

The Extent of the Problem

A few years ago I had a conversation with the senior nursing officer in a large general hospital. One of the interesting points she made during our discussion was how concerned she was about absenteeism. I asked, 'How bad is it?'

She replied: 'We don't know.' The subsequent conversation

went something like this: 'If you don't know how bad it is,
then why are you worried?'
   'We're worried because we know *it must be pretty bad.'*
   'Why don't you measure it?'
   'We don't like to, just in case the figures are really as bad
as we think they might be.'
   I then offered to help her carry out a quick measurement
exercise. But that idea was no good either and the response
to that suggestion was: 'We would rather you didn't do that.
Our trades unions might not like it very much.'

In many ways, that conversation encapsulates the whole
problem. Many organizations don't like to admit that they
suffer from absenteeism. A great number of them are prepared to discuss it at great length but not to initiate actions
or policies to cure it. Not nearly enough are prepared to
analyse the causes and then put together an organized cam-
paign for dealing with them.

An occupational health specialist once told me that, in
his opinion, the people who contribute to surveys on absenteeism tend to be managers who are doing something about
the problem. He thought that, by definition (or certainly by
implication), Britain's absenteeism problems may actually
be far *worse* than the figures would suggest.

The moral is very simple: *If you won't admit you have it,*
it's very difficult to cure it.

It has been suggested that absenteeism costs British industry somewhere in the region of five thousand million pounds
a year. These figures come not from the author but from
the Confederation of British Industry. As a comparison,
where 200m working days a year are lost through absenteeism, only around 40m working days are lost through industrial action. The problem is not just about stopping people
from walking out, it's actually about getting them to turn
up in the first place!

It is also worth noting that our perception of the 'image'
of organizations is frequently influenced by the demeanour
or behaviour of staff.

Recently I visited a restaurant, part of a national chain

MOUNT-PLEASANT LIBRARY
TEL. 051 207 3581 Ext. 3701 .

which is well known on almost every major road. The notice inside the restaurant doorway said: 'Owing to staff shortages, only half the restaurant is available for use today. Management deeply regrets any inconvenience caused to our patrons.' You may consider that a statement which says that only half the restaurant is open owing to 'staff shortages' also implies that the patrons are likely to receive half the service as well. After ten minutes I concluded this was right, so I left and bought a sandwich elsewhere.

It is also worth remembering that organizations which suffer from staff shortages (or, if you prefer it, inability to manage attendance effectively), also appear to have endemic 'morale' problems, while the demeanour and behaviour of those staff who are left trying to cope with the effects of poor attenders are there for all to see.

At a hotel recently, when I was trying to check out, I was confronted by the sight of one receptionist trying to cope with a long queue of exasperated guests. After 15 minutes waiting I reached my turn and asked her in (largely one-way) conversation what was the problem. She could hardly bring herself to answer, but shen she did, she simply muttered: 'Staff shortages.' When I asked her what that meant, she said in the same undertone: 'Everybody away sick. Next please.'

At a high nightly guest rate this does not fill the potential guest with optimism or enthusiasm. It simply encourages him or her to go and look for an alternative the following night.

Absenteeism isn't something that's confined to a few sectors of the economy. It's everywhere – private sector and public sector, manufacturing and service. It's much more serious than it looks. It's a cost problem, it's uncompetitive, and it's a measure of efficiency. It causes overtime, late deliveries and dissatisfied customers. And everybody's got it. Of course, some employers have more of it than others, but there is little point in pretending that it's simply something that happens to other organizations. Ignoring it is short-sighted. Absenteeism is like fungus. It thrives in dark corners and the more you leave it, the more it spreads.

What Can You Do about It?

If we were to believe some prophets of doom and gloom, we would have to assume that, without profound and far-reaching changes in the law of employment, nothing can be done about absenteeism. Such people argue that it is a question of abolishing Employment Protection and the Contracts of Employment Act; provided that such restrictive pieces of law were removed, they say, controlling employees' behaviour would be much easier. Well, perhaps it would be, but so would abusing them.

Experience shows that you cannot punish your way out of trouble. Commonsense necessitates that whatever changes are eventually made to the law, absenteeism or, to put it more positively, attendance is an issue which is going to have to be *managed* if it is to become a plus point in any company's track record.

There are a number of key factors:

- The need to make work a good place to attend
- The need to ensure that line managers and supervisors are held accountable for behaviour as well as performance
- The need to make 'people management' part of the appraisal system wherever it exists, and 'people skills' part of the selection, induction and training policy
- The need to make managers and supervisors responsible for absence control, and to use personnel specialists as the means for facilitating this
- The need to train, coach and counsel line managers and supervisors in communication techniques which enable them to cope effectively with their role in counselling and providing support
- The need to keep accurate records so that absence can be spotted as a small problem before it becomes a big issue
- The need to stop relying upon false motivators such as attendance bonus schemes which never really solve the problem
- The need to be realistic; if you have got the rate down to 2%, you *are* controlling it and doing rather well.

Much of this book is about practical actions that managers can take. It is for the personnel specialists who may read this to help them take these actions and to provide them with the necessary training and assistance. In this way, they will enable line managers to accept their accountability for managing people, as well as managing products or procedures.

Chapter 2
Prime Causes

Commonsense insists that there have to be millions of instances in which people simply don't feel needed, believe they won't be missed or simply have something more important to do. The recent Director of the Industrial Society, John Garnett, used to say: 'The challenge, when people wake up at 7 o'clock on Monday morning and their eyes flicker on the pillow, and they are lying in bed wondering whether to be another absence statistic or not, is to persuade them to give the benefit of the doubt to their jobs rather than their beds.' He always used to go on to say that he was referring not to chronic illness but to the kind of illness that people felt at 7 o'clock on Monday morning, because it was his experience that if they somehow dragged themselves to work, then they invariably felt better by 11 o'clock!

Britain is a world leader in its standards of living. It has one of the finest health services in the world, whatever its critics say about it, and its control of illness and disease is second to very few, if any, countries. Yet Britain continues to suffer from a chronic absentee problem. Many observers are beginning to ask themselves how much of this absence is the result of real illness or disability. Of course, most of the reasons given for absence are about illness, back ache, stomach pains, 'flu symptoms and so forth. But there have to be many occasions when employees claim to be suffering from various illnesses when in fact they have simply opted out of work and could have opted in.

What causes this? What is it about the working environment that apparently causes people to feel unable to face it on so many occasions?

Occupational health specialists have discovered that there are numerous major influences on absenteeism. Among the many factors which stem from either social, organizational or personal influences, however, it is important to understand that only three of them are strictly 'medical'. These are epidemics, environmental hazards and medical conditions.

There are, however, a whole host of other influences, including

- climate
- overtime
- Social Security arrangements
- health services available
- social attitudes
- the nature of the work
- the size of the company
- industrial relations
- personnel policy
- Sick Pay
- the quality of supervision
- working conditions
- age
- sex
- job satisfaction
- personality traits
- alcohol
- family responsibilities
- travel arrangements
- social activities.

Let's take a closer look at the key reasons which, in my experience, influence attendance – and attendance policies.

The Nature of Work

A great deal of work is very boring indeed. It doesn't matter what people say about job enrichment, enlargement or redesign, the problem is that a number of occupations are, if there is such a word, 'unenrichable'. Consequently large numbers of people are confronted with the gloomy reality of having to turn up day in, day out for their entire lives to do a job which is repetitive, maybe dirty, invariably uninteresting and frequently appears to lack any sense of purpose. The alternatives are no better: unemployment, similar employment or worse employment.

I once visited a food processing company which employed a fairly large number of women (mainly part time) to disembowel chickens, which passed before them in endless quantities. The smell was awful, absenteeism commensurately high.

'What could you do about it?' asked the Personnel Manager.

'What about talking to them?' said I. He was incredulous.

'Talk to them? Don't be ridiculous.'

Yet when he and I did talk to them, they didn't think the job was so bad. They liked the companionship. Spirits were high. But the real reason they stayed away was that their managers had so much contempt for them that they hardly spoke to them except to tell them to speed up. One of them said: 'They treat us just like the chickens.'

The problem was that the managers had given up. They hated the environment so much themselves that they assumed the same applied to the employees.

This may be a somewhat exaggerated example, but it does make the point. And, of course, there are millions of jobs which, if not specifically unpleasant, are nontheless not what their holders would have chosen. The educational system does not prepare people for a lifetime of boredom and drudgery.

But the nature of the work is not simply a question of boredom or carrying out unpleasant tasks. It is also about environment. Take, for example, the nursing profession, where it is difficult to retain commitment or a sense of urgency if you're surrounded by stressful scenes and, at the same time, confronted by the prospect of wards being closed because administrators are trying to cut costs.

Teachers faced with over-large classes, while schools elsewhere are being closed, have the same kinds of problems. Retail employees who work on the checkouts at superstores, coping day in and day out with endless queues of customers, all of them with barrows which are filled to the brim, must inevitably sometimes wonder what life is all about.

Time, political and environmental pressures all conspire in their various ways to undermine people's sense of urgency, and this in turn is reflected in their behaviour. Sometimes it all gets too much and the easiest thing to do is give yourself a rest.

The Size of the Organization

As organizations get bigger and bigger, it becomes more and more difficult for individuals to feel that they matter or to see where they fit into the scheme of things. At the top of the organization it is always crystal clear who works for whom and how much you matter. If you are missing, the Managing Director misses you or somebody of 'equal standing'.

However, when you work at the bottom, the question of whether or not anybody misses you is a far more nebulous one. It is all very well, as somebody once said, saying to employees that they will not be treated as just so many cogs in a wheel. But when they can see 85 other cogs next to them, it's very difficult to believe it.

Small family businesses tend not to have absentee problems. Large public utilities do. Whatever other differences there may be between the two, one fact is difficult to dispute. In small firms everybody needs each other and understands where he or she fits in. In the second case, it is sometimes extremely difficult to tell whether either of those assertions is true.

Personnel Policy

In my experience, some of the problems are caused by personnel policy. One of the major difficulties in managing attendance lies in measuring it accurately enough. In almost every organization, some absence is regarded as acceptable, frequently without any form of medical evidence. The level of acceptability varies, but it needs to be faced that a number of personnel policies effectively encourage people to take time off. Such policies include:

- only taking action when a certain 'trigger point' is reached, e.g. absence without an acceptable explanation on five separate occasions
- paying attendance bonuses, which simply become accepted as part of the total remuneration package and do very little more than restrict absenteeism to somewhere around a barely acceptable level (see Chapter 4)
- over-participation by personnel specialists in the management process; the result is that supervisors and managers become inclined to opt out, and are only too happy to leave absence control to somebody else, even if that somebody can't actually be held accountable for it.

The Quality of Supervision

Supervision is the single most influential factor in managing attendance. We'll return to this subject later but, for the time being, let it be said that it is the *personal* relationship between managers, supervisors and their teams which has the biggest effect on commitment, whether that is measured in terms of attendance, time keeping, quality, quantity, time or cost. Wherever supervision fails to build such a relationship, commitment problems inevitably follow. Conversely, when people believe they're needed, they put up with a great deal.

A 16-year-old apprentice went on one of the Sail Training Association's tall ships for a week's course. When he returned, he was asked how he had enjoyed it and he replied: 'It was awful. I was sick all the time. I was freezing cold. I was also soaking wet and didn't eat anything for about four days.'

Yet when asked if he would recommend other people to go, he unhesitatingly replied: 'Of course.' When asked why, he went on to explain that what he had really learnt was the need not to let your colleagues down. The person who had made him believe this was important was the person in charge of his watch. He had explained in his own way that everybody was suffering from sea sickness, that the ship had to be manned, that eventually things would get better, and that if you opted out it only meant that somebody else was going to have to do your job as well as his or her own.

Family Responsibilities and Travel Arrangements

Many absentees are people confronted daily with the problems of managing other commitments besides their responsibility to the 'work ethic'. Such people include mothers of large families, single parents and only children who have elderly parents for whom to care.

Sometimes the arrangements they have to make to cope with such responsibilities go wrong. Child minders go sick. Children become ill. The elderly require extra help. Maybe travel arrangements become difficult because train times are changed or some enterprising-planner moves the bus stop or changes a timetable without having reference to the individual's particular needs.

When these things happen, some employees find it very difficult to cope. They may still have their responsibilities, but if ignorant managers and supervisors don't support them in coping with the difficulties which they have to face on a daily basis, then from time to time, they will run away from them and plead sickness, rather than explain the truth and ask for help.

So while it is clear that medical causes have their place in absence statistics, it would be naive to assume that every time somebody is away, he or she is prevented from attending by the traditional reasons like influenza symptoms, back ache or stomach pains. It would, however, be equally naive to believe that such people are always away because they are lazy.

Commonsense Influences

So absence is not just a question of illness or disability. The reality is that, while a few of us are lucky enough to believe so much in our work that we simply live for it, for many, many more it is the other way around. They have to work in order to live. They do very ordinary jobs – jobs which are difficult to enrich and impossible to redesign. (Frequently they are managed by ordinary people, who themselves were not appointed because of any kind of innate ability to inspire and motivate others.) They are prisoners of the system. For them, work is always there – every day, every week, month in month out, for their entire working lives.

It doesn't do a great deal of good to talk to such people about the challenge of 'creating wealth', in order to pay for the goods and services that the rest of us enjoy. Such talk is very persuasive in conference halls, but it doesn't work quite so well when you are standing in a swamp with alligators biting at the backs of your legs.

The easiest way to opt out, from time to time, is to 'go sick'. It is worth remembering that when people feel off colour they sometimes mix up physical symptoms with their emotions. To do so is human and, as we ought to acknowledge, absenteeism is about human beings being human.

Talking of being human, it is also human to be lazy. And it should not be forgotten that there are a number of instances in which people do not go to work simply because they don't feel like going to work. They have something better to do. The something better might be a social engagement, a football match, a lover or any one of a number of better alternative pursuits.

One organization that I know well has a factory near a very large race course. It used to find that its absence figures increased every time there was a race meeting. As a result of a sustained effort by line managers and supervisors to challenge such casual absences, it doesn't have the problem any longer. It's all a question of facing up to the unpalatable!

Statutory Sick Pay

Many excuses are made for high absence rates; one of the latest is the one which says 'If we didn't have SSP procedures and self-certification, the problem would not be nearly so bad.' Sometimes believers in this argument imply that self-certification encourages more long-term sickness. You just write out your own medical certificate and stay off for as long as you want . . .

It would be difficult to prove that SSP didn't have some influence on absenteeism. But most instances of sickness are not long term. They tend to last three days or less and are just what they always used to be before self-certification was introduced. Originally, in order to qualify for Sickness Benefit as administered by the British Government, it was necessary to produce medical evidence of your incapacity after three days' sickness. Consequently, many employees used simply to take off 2–3 days every time. Realists have to ask themselves 'What's changed?'

At the end of the day, people will believe what they want to believe. I have not yet been persuaded that SSP and self-certification are the main cause of Britain's 5%. But it is true that SSP procedures present managers with an *opportunity*: to get closer to attendance problems and tackle them before they become major obstacles.

Genuine Incapacity

Finally, it has to be remembered that some people do from time to time suffer from genuine illness or incapacity. It would be quite wrong to assume that every absentee has some kind of family commitment, is lazy or bored to death. People do catch influenza, have operations, break legs and suffer from various other incapacitating conditions.

There are two very important morals to this short point. The first is: don't assume a thing. The second: if we take the maximum amount of interest in employees, we are more likely to know whether their absence from work is caused by genuine factors or by others which need, and indeed merit, much further investigation.

Chapter 3
Measurement

How many managers – or even personnel managers – *know* the absence rates (attendance rates if they're really positive) in their organizations? How many people could make an accurate comparison between one department and another? How many managers are aware that employees are away more often under one supervisor than under another?

The exact answers don't matter – because there is *never* enough awareness of these issues. And until everyone knows, the problem will never be effectively managed.

The real problem is that not nearly enough people believe that absence is a problem. One of the first steps in managing it is to be able to present persuasive proof that it exists.

How to Calculate Absenteeism

1. Calculate the total number of available working days in the period concerned (e.g. no. of working days in one month): 21 (note: you obviously have to exclude Saturdays, Sundays and national holidays)

Number of employees = 18

Total days available = 378

2. Calculate total days missed by individuals during the period, excluding authorized holidays, e.g. 29

3. Calculate percentage rate for absenteeism (total days absent divided by total days available multiplied by 100)

Gross absence = 7.67%

Making Comparisons

Once you've established a formula for measuring the extent of the problem, start making comparisons – or contrasts. It is infinitely worthwhile to compare horizontally as well as vertically. Much statistical evidence already exists to prove, for example, that managers are hardly ever away from work, that staff are away more than managers, and hourly paid workers more than staff. Those are results we might even expect.

But what about comparisons between *similar* employees? Why do hourly paid people in one department stay away more than hourly paid in another? Why is 'sickness' endemic in Data Processing – but not in Accounts? Is it worse at night than during the day? Are there any interesting age comparisons? Sex trends? Differences in attendance patterns between ethnic groups?

These are all questions which personnel managers should be able to answer, so that they can bring them to line managers' attention. However, you do have to be able to measure the problem in the first place – so the calculation formula is very useful.

Keeping Records

Don't argue about whose job it is to keep the records until you've established a record-keeping system. The reason for this seemingly obvious piece of advice is a little more subtle than it seems. It is only when you *try* to put together a centrally controlled record-keeping system that you begin to understand how impractical it is to maintain. Recording statistics is all very well: clock cards, time sheets and other similar paperwork will always provide information about how many people are at work, where attendance is best, which areas are a potential – or current – problem. But record keeping is more than simple 'number crunching'. We also need to know *why* people are away, *who*'s responsible for them, *what* reasons they gave, *what* the company did to provide help, support or advice, and *how* local management and supervision dealt with the incident.

There is no way in the world that personnel managers can do all of that, although few would deny that it's all relevant information. It is information, however, which cannot be recorded centrally and must be treated as a departmental responsibility involving managers and supervisors as well.

Designing an effective record-keeping system has some useful by-products. Perhaps the most important is that it underlines who is really accountable for the problem – and its solutions: managers and supervisors.

Some years ago, in a Glasgow shipbuilders, the General Manager published a 'league table' of attendance under each supervisor's name. This table indicated very clearly that riggers, riveters, fitters etc. were inclined to attend more often in some parts of the yard than in others.

When he published these interesting comparisons, supervisors protested and said to do so was invidious – perhaps even victimization. The General Manager simply said 'Why?'

'Well,' said the union representative for the supervisors, 'you're showing people up – and that's not fair.'

'Exactly,' said the manager. 'I'm showing up who's good at getting people to come to work. Attendance is what I'm interested in, not absenteeism. And this yard depends on attendance.'

Not much to argue about there. What is interesting in this example is the way in which the theme was positive. Sadly, many companies are driven by negative statistics: 'Rejects,' 'Accidents,' 'Complaints' and 'Absenteeism' – instead of 'Goods right first time,' 'Safety,' 'Customer satisfaction,' and 'Attendance.' It's back to comparisons between half-empty bottles and half-full ones – but the difference is very important when you take the first steps in controlling absence.

If people have to defend statistics, they will *be* defensive. They'll fudge, evade, lie and cheat in order to wriggle out of the problem – because the statistics made them feel defensive in the first place. When people don't like messages they blame both message and messenger. So publish the statistics in positive terms – your colleagues may be more prepared to talk to you about them.

What to Include/Exclude in the Records

Include absolutely everything except authorized holidays. Include part-timers as well as full-timers. Include even casuals if they're casuals upon whom the business in some way relies.

The reason for this all-embracing approach is simple. If you don't know the extent of the problem, you can never manage it. Perhaps you've noticed the way people protest about the figures: 'I know it's running at 7½% but if it wasn't for Tom's heart attack or Fred's operation it wouldn't be so bad.' For two pins such people would exclude Tom and Fred from the statistics. They could be missing for months before anybody worried about them. The issue isn't about disciplining them – it's about managing the business, caring for Fred and Tom and looking after the interests of their colleagues.

So include everything – however much you're tempted into omissions, don't be talked into falsifying the statistics in order to protect egos or avoid offence. People are either *at* work or *away* from work. And if you present incorrect or misleading data, don't be surprised if you make the wrong decisions. As many people have frequently proved, one exception always leads to another – and another . . .

Indirect Measurement – Opinion Polls, Attitude Surveys, etc.

There are a number of conflicting views about the best ways of measuring attitudes and behaviour. In my experience, however, the most effective way of finding out what is bad about an organization is by looking in the first instance at what is *good*!

Some years ago I was asked by a distribution company to examine and provide advice about a labour turnover problem. I spent some weeks going through endless exit interview records, analysing every conceivable angle and writing down comprehensive lists of possible reasons – environmental, economic, socio-economic, etc.

Finally, my own boss asked me why I was spending so much time on the problem. I told him what I was doing and he simply snorted: 'Good God! Stop wasting everybody's time. Go and find 50 people who've stayed longer than 12 months and ask them why they haven't left. That will tell you why people leave.'

He was right. It did. In the same way, the best way of finding out what causes bad *attendance is to observe what happens wherever there's* good *attendance. In such environments you learn more about what can be done in practical terms to safeguard motivation and maximize it.*

Other useful sources of information about attendance patterns are company employee surveys, opinion polls, etc. Try looking, for example, at company communications. A very good indication of other trends is to find out what people need to understand and want to know and then to check and see whether they find it out and who tells them. Employees who don't know how well they're doing, don't know what's expected of them, don't talk with their supervisor, also don't feel part of a team and invariably show less commitment to their employer; that, in turn, shows up in a variety of ways, not least of them being quality, quantity, cost and behaviour.

MOUNT PLEASANT LIBRARY
TEL. 051 207 3581 Ext. 3701 .

Chapter 4
Absenteeism and Personnel Specialists

Many companies depend upon personnel managers as the means of controlling their attendance policies. Personnel managers are the experts on sickness, discipline and counselling procedures and inevitably become the guardians of a company's integrity and reputation. They are the bridge between managers and trade union representatives. They are regarded as welfare specialists and lawyers and, by definition, they also play a vital part in the success of these top organizations, many of which depend crucially on sound personnel policies.

Such companies do exist. Almost everybody has heard of examples such as IBM, Mars, Nissan, etc. Without doubt, there are significantly more than these. But what they all have in common is that the personnel function does not attempt to manage people on its own. On the contrary, it does everything within its power to delegate the responsibility for employee motivation back to the line, where it actually belongs.

Why fudge the issue? Without any question, the responsibility for absence control should rest with line managers. Only line managers can be held accountable for people's performance, and it is quite wrong that their actions should be controlled by or subject to personnel managers, however well-intentioned they may be.

This is not to say that personnel managers don't make a contribution. Nobody can replace them in ensuring that a sense of balance and consistency of behaviour are maintained. Frequently, personnel managers are also the company experts on employment law. They know the procedures inside out, or they should do. And, for these reasons, it is crucial that they are closely involved in the whole process of managing individuals whose behaviour does not always conform with the standards laid down.

This does not mean that they should be held accountable. On the contrary, it is their job to ensure that proper accountabilities are met elsewhere; there is, of course, a subtle difference between the two.

In a major multinational manufacturer in Great Britain, the ultimate responsibility for dismissal continues to remain with the personnel function. Absenteeism in its plants varies between 4 and 6%. This means that in some departments the rate is as low as 1½–2% while in others it attains as much as 6½–7%. The departments with the low averages are those to which personnel department has consciously divested its responsibility to strong line managers.

Yet positive influence from personnel specialists is, beyond almost any dispute, *the* crucial factor in managing absenteeism in the workplace. Yes, controlling it is a line-management responsibility. Certainly, motivation is the job of the immediate boss. Of course, when employees don't come in, personnel shouldn't take all the blame. So what kind of role do personnel managers have?

Establishing Accountability for People

Much success in business is due to both original *and* creative thinking. Sir Frank Whittle may have invented the jet engine – but somebody else improved on the idea later. There wasn't a great deal to copy. The same can be said about electric light, the internal combustion engine, the computer, space travel or even the baked bean. All of them were created from one person's idea and developed by others, intent on turning a good notion into a better one, polished and adapted by still more people.

Ideas are conceptual, i.e. by definition original. People who own problems think of ways of solving them. Other

people help to develop them. In modern times the breadth
of management accountability has got ever wider, and now
often includes engineering support, maybe quality control
(not assurance), research and development, cost control,
budgeting and many more functions that used to be managed by specialists. This does not make managers experts
on all these areas. It does, however, make them accountable
for them. Because they own the problem, they first have to
understand it, and then make a sensible contribution
towards solving it, be that through research, planning, selection, structure or organization.

Nobody comes along and says to such managers: 'This is
your problem – and this is what I'm going to do about it
for you' – not in modern organizations with a bright and
forward-looking competitive approach to business. These
days specialists say: 'Let's achieve a joint understanding of
this problem and settle on what *you*'re going to do about
it' (except in the matter of managing people, where for
some reason the responsibilities are still badly defined).

There are hundreds and thousands of managers and
supervisors – maybe millions – who still don't seem to understand what it is that motivates people at work. Hundreds
and thousands of managers who create (or allow to be
created) conditions which do nothing for employee motivation except undermine it, and who apply or implement the
solutions offered by personnel specialists with cynicism or
disbelief (I don't know which is worse) or perhaps with half-
hearted effort, but all too rarely with simple enthusiasm.

Why is this? The answer is very straightforward. They
don't *own* the problem. In the past 20 years, during a career
in business, the public sector, private sector, various insti-
tutional bodies and as a management consultant in virtually
every part of our industrial society, I have met only a handful of managers whose objective (upon which their career
and security depended) was to achieve measured and agreed
standards of employee motivation and attendance.

Cut the cost by 10%? Yes. Install new plant that nobody
has ever made work before? Certainly. Achieve new quality

standards? Of course. But ensure attendance doesn't fall below 97%? That's different!

Yet the paradox is plain to see. It's line managers who create the problems (well, most of the time, anyhow!). But it's personnel managers who think of the solutions, some right and some of them convoluted – but all of them with the same basic flaw. They come from the wrong source.

So where does this leave the personnel specialist? It's a bit strange, in a book published by the Institute of Personnel Management, to find such an 'attack' on the very people who will read it. But, of course, this isn't an attack; it's a statement of fact. The problem is with line management; in their efforts to provide support, personnel specialists have not always tackled the issue in the right way.

To illustrate the point, look at these two examples of conversations at work:

Personnel Manager: *We have a real absence problem in your department, George.*

Manager: *I know, lazy so and so's.*

Personnel Manager: *Well, it's running at 5% – that means they're all away for about an extra two working weeks a year.*

Manager: *It isn't that bad, surely?*

Personnel Manager: *It is, I'm afraid. I've worked out the figures.*

Manager: *Well, you're the expert. What should I do about it?*

Personnel Manager: *What I think we should do is set up a counselling programme . . .*

Already the plan is going awry. The personnel manager has identified the problem – and now he's posing the solution. He hasn't even convinced his colleague of its extent. He hasn't established any accountability and, any minute now, the manager is going to place an objection in the way. A good bet would be that he'll say: 'I'm a bit snowed under at the moment', 'Tell me who they are' or 'I'm not sure those figures stack up.'

The delaying process will already have commenced.

Now consider this approach:

Personnel Manager: *Do you think you have an absence problem, George?*
Manager: *'Well, hasn't everybody?*
Personnel Manager: *Well, that's true. But I think if you check your rates, you'll find you have a problem which undermines your production targets.*
Manager: *Check the rates? Isn't that your job?*
Personnel Manager: *No, it's yours. Are you going to send me a bouquet when you hit your budget this year?*
Manager: *What's that got to do with you?*
Personnel Manager: *My job is to help you hit it, George. And you won't do that if all your chaps are going to be away for an extra fortnight this year.*
Manager: *Extra fortnight? What* are *you talking about?*
Personnel Manager: *Let's just do this calculation together and then we'll discuss what you think you should do about it . . .*

Establish the ownership of the problem in the first place and the solutions will inevitably begin to flow – from the *right* source. They might, of course, be wrong – but the way is clear to start turning the wrong solutions into right ones, and good ones into better ones. Instead of being some kind of 'expert', the personnel specialist becomes a source of advice. He or she remains a facilitator, a support – but first establishes the fundamental accountability. That's the first step. Unless it is clearly decided, personnel managers will always find themselves thinking up solutions to someone else's problem.

Training Managers and Supervisors

Most managers are appointed for technical reasons. They are professionally qualified – either as scientists or technologists, salesmen or marketing specialists, engineers or administrators. They aren't selected because they are primarily communicators or motivators. Obviously such factors are sometimes taken into account in the selection process, but they aren't usually determining factors and are almost never fundamental issues. It isn't practical to cross people off short lists because they aren't born leaders.

Managers, therefore, must be ready to be trained, coached and equipped to deal with motivation problems. Yet in many organizations, this subject, perhaps the most important in management development, is tackled too late, if at all, handled unprofessionally by in-house trainers, who have insufficient credibility, or skated over as part of a general management training programme. It's far too important for this – and personnel management, therefore, has a vital role to play in ensuring that it is provided for.

Every manager needs to know:

- what people want and expect from work
- the barriers to achieving commitment
- the actions that need to be taken to provide for motivation and commitment.

What People Want and Expect from Work
It is not difficult to list their minimum requirements:

- to work in a clean and pleasing environment
- to know what is expected of them and be part of a team
- to know how well they're doing
- to know how they can improve
- to believe their security is provided for
- to be paid fairly
- to be recognized and appreciated
- to have the opportunity for putting forward their views and experience
- to have their grievances fairly dealt with.

There may be a great deal more than this. But what we know is that whenever those factors are missing, motivation suffers. People might not stop work – but they do stop *working*. They drift away – or go sick.

The Barriers to Commitment

Commitment is always measurable. It shows up in timekeeping, attendance, quality, safety, industrial relations disputes, administrative standards, customer care. You name it – and the attitude of employees will show up in it. Tackle any visible sign of poor commitment and a host of other indicators will improve as well.

The major barriers are:

SIZE – remoteness, scattered groups, large working groups, no teams, no bosses

IGNORANCE ABOUT WHAT IS EXPECTED – everybody needs to know what his or her boss wants him to achieve

OVER-RELIANCE ON REWARDS – money frequently undermines, occasionally motivates but never does the job on its own

The Actions that Provide for Motivation and Commitment

Managers who hope to motivate their staff need to provide a number of basic conditions:

- clearly defined objectives
- teams and teamwork
- regular performance review
- communications
- consultation and involvement
- good management–union relations
- conditions of employment applied as fairly and justly as possible.

Again, there may be many more – but this handful of actions is a good start. Personnel managers who don't ensure that managers can deliver them simply reap what they sow.

Objective Setting

Every organization claims to have objectives – and so, at the very top, many of them do. But this is often not nearly enough. If we believe that employees need to know what's expected of them, then we must accept that it's of little use simply telling them what is in the budget, even supposing such a document is truthful and reliable!

Budgets, business plans and corporate objectives have to be broken down into a raft of supporting projects and targets at *every* level. Once this has happened, teams can see what they're shooting for – and it's teamwork and team spirit which play a major part in achieving the sense of urgency and importance that successful organizations invariably boast about.

Teams and Teamwork

Much glib talk goes on about 'teamwork'. One company I know, which is full of casual itinerant labour, has an appalling safety record and even in these days of unemployment suffers a high turnover of employees, is always referring to its 'team' approach. Presumably some of its customers even believe it!

Effective teams, however, are dependent on structure and size, common objectives and collective involvement. If they're not about these things, they're not about anything. Personnel Managers can do a great deal to ensure that:

Every workgroup has its own permanent *boss*

Every team is of a manageable size (the best experience can be summed up in what is blasphemously called the 'Jesus' principle, i.e. the maximum should be 12)

Every team has a common goal(s)

Every team communicates regularly about what has to be achieved.

Ensuring that these things happen is a subtle process. Tell managers to do them and they probably won't. Require managers to build teams and ask them to come up with ways of doing it – and maybe they will. At that stage it becomes simply a coaching problem.

Performance Review

Sometimes known as appraisal, this process is one of the most maligned and abused in the human resources 'dictionary'. How can managers talk to their teams about how well or badly they're doing, if they themselves don't know the answer to the question?

It is not a matter of establishing reams of paperwork and forms to provide for effective performance reviews. It's a question of establishing, at the level of every functional head, a means of ensuring that each manages his or her own system for *objectively* reviewing performance at every level. Too often, appraisal is regarded as an ordeal or a way of justifying the salary levels of managers. But every one of us needs to know how well or badly we are doing. All we are seeking is information.

Managing Communications

Here we touch on the hoary subject of employee communication – surely the biggest chapter in the history of instant 'plug in' solutions. There are very few managers who don't believe that teamwork and motivation – the factors upon which good attendance depends – depend on regular and relevant employee communication methods. But there are even fewer who could with any real truth claim to be regular and relevant communicators. This is not the place to embark upon an exhaustive review of the various communication solutions known to man. It is, however, worth taking a quick look at some actions which have been known to work.

In a road haulage company recently, one supervisor decided to take matters into his own hands. Faced with an absence problem of some 17% in his section, he held a briefing session and asked his team if it was surprised to learn that they were the sickest group in the region.

The response was quite dramatic. One member of the team said: 'Why are you getting at us? What you need to do is talk to the people who are causing the problem.' The supervisor's reply was: 'I might just do that, but I thought, in the meantime, one or two of you might discuss it among yourselves as well.' Two weeks later his absence problem was down to 6%, a month later to 5%.

The moral is very simple: if you want to solve the problem – get the ownership right in the first place, then talk to the people who are causing it.

In a British automotive manufacturer, a few years ago, absence in one part of the plant was running a rate of between 35 and 40%. A manager decided to take matters into his own hands and went out on to the shop floor in order to discuss the problem with some of the culprits, so to speak. Among the first few people he talked to were two fitters. The conversation went like this:

Manager: *Do you think there's an absence problem here?*
Fitter No. 1: *No, not really. There might be a few people off from time to time, but no, not really a problem.*
Manager: *Well do you know that the absence rate in the department is current running at 40%?*
Fitter: *Is that so?*
Manager (nonplussed): *Well, do you know what 40% means?*
Fitter: *No, haven't a clue.*
Fitter No. 2: *Well, what it actually means is that sometime during the next 10 days, you are going to be off for 4 of them.*
Fitter No. 1: *How do you know? I haven't decided yet how many days I'm going to take off during the next 10.*

Readers will note that the issue of whether or not this employee was going to take time off work had nothing at all to do with the employer for whom he was working, but solely with a question of whether or not there was something better to do!

This particular company had tried to solve the problem over a matter of months, first of all by publishing absence figures and statistics regularly in the works newspaper. It had

*tried discussing the matter with its trade unions and it had
also reiterated through noticeboards and bulletins the number
of motor cars that the company had failed to deliver as a
result of absenteeism. None of these reminders had done any
good at all.*

*The first-line supervisors eventually came up with the sol-
ution. They simply said: 'Why won't you let us talk to them?
You have tried everything else.'*

*The company took the advice and the very next week
briefing groups on the shop floor took place, at which foremen explained simply what happened when you didn't come
in. They explained this in language which was best suited to
them and their teams, and no doubt the words that they used
would not have been approved by senior executives. But they
got their message across.*

*The net result, over the next few months, was that absentee-
ism gradually went down. The last time I discussed the problem with them, the rate was significantly lower than in other
plants with which the company could fairly make a
comparison.*

*In another organization which employed large numbers of
female workers who were engaged on particularly repetitive
assembly work, the absence rate used to run at similarly
disturbing levels. I can remember visiting this organization
and being conducted round it by a personnel manager who
explained to me that such employees were a good investment,
because they were only women and liked working for pin
money.*

*So saying, he took me into a large room which was filled
with these unfortunate ladies, sitting glumly by conveyor
belts, which moved before them bearing junction boxes, tran-
sistors and other mysterious items.*

*I introduced myself to one employee and asked her what
she was making. She said: 'It's called an xz/12.' I then asked
what the said 'xz/12' actually achieved, where it fitted into
the product and what its significance was. The employee said
that she didn't know. So then I asked how long she had been
making it, and she said about five years.*

At this point we both saw the irony and seeing our laughter, the checker – a man in a white coat pacing up and down at the side of the room, policing the operation – asked us what the joke was. My friend simply said: 'This bloke here has just asked what this thing does and I couldn't tell him. So I told him I had been making them for five years and we both thought that was silly! Anyhow what does *it do?'*

The reply of the checker should be recorded in memoriam *as a tribute to the millions of people who have been condemned over the years to working for 'pin money'. He said: 'I don't know, I only check 'em.'*

I subsequently talked to the personnel managers on this plant and asked them whether they thought that the fact that people didn't know the significance of their jobs had anything to do with the extraordinarily high absence rate, high even for female labour employed on a casual basis in the area. They had not even considered the issue and weren't much inclined to do so either.

Yet our commonsense and experience insists that the enthusiastic and systematic communication of such fundamental issues *has* to have a profound effect upon the commitment of employees.

Achieving a Positive Attitude to Conditions of Employment

Employees are not stupid. Come up with a spurious plan to persuade them to come to work, or work harder, and they'll come up with a better one of their own. For many years management has been baffled or intrigued by the ability of employees to earn production bonuses without appearing to actually *work* any harder.

So don't expect that fiddling around with wages structures or payment systems will always promote a greater sense of motivation – unless, of course, they were wrong and unjust in the first place.

A service organization with a massive labour-turnover and absenteeism problem appointed a new Chief Executive. He discovered that wage levels were monstrously out of line with those in similar industries and re-adjusted them; at the same time, he rectified a number of other injustices. The result was an immediate improvement in both attendance and labour retention.

However, rectifying injustice is one thing, perpetrating it is quite another – and to pay people a 'bonus' for attendance (i.e. for turning up to work before they do any) is as invidious an employment practice as any.

Remember Herzberg, who pointed out quite correctly that many conditions of employment can as easily demotivate as motivate. Personnel managers should at least ensure that those in their organization are compatible with high performance!

Managing Trade Unions

Personnel managers can make an enormous contribution in ensuring that employee representatives understand and, if possible, are involved in absence control. Appendices 2 and 5 show how this may be achieved, while Chapter 7 offers more general guidance on the issue.

Recognizing Good Attendance

Saying 'well done' to good attenders is a rare but simple piece of management weaponry. Once again, personnel managers can have a profound influence in this context by encouraging line managers to thank employees who show their support by turning up for work consistently – and, presumably, from time to time in difficult circumstances.

A line manager in a manufacturing company writes a personal letter to 100% (or nearly) attenders and simply says: 'I want to personally thank you for your support.'

An office-equipment manufacturer presents small awards

to good attenders. The awards are deliberately scaled down and are no more than a token of good will.

Chapter 5
The Role of Line Managers and Supervisors

Attendance – and certainly the control of it – is management's responsibility and, as we have seen, there is no way in the world that personnel managers can be held directly accountable for the behaviour of employees. On the bottom line, if managers want the credit for the achievements of their teams when they are doing well, they have to be prepared to take the blame for factors within their control which undermine performance.

A great many managers find the question of absenteeism embarrassing. They don't find it easy to discuss personal problems, so frequently they prefer to ignore the issue. Further complications (such as the fear of industrial tribunals and the role of trade union representatives who, quite understandably, take a protective stance) don't make life any easier.

The problem, however, is not likely to go away; however much managers would like to abdicate their responsibility, they can't – provided that personnel managers won't let them. It is frequently the case, however, that absence control is not officially delegated to managers. Instead the position is left unclear, so matters can quickly get out of control.

Thus, when employees decide that they are unable to come to work, they telephone the company's switchboard, a personnel clerk or some administrative department or other. Their message is taken by somebody who has simply nothing at all to do with the problem and (it could often be said) cares even less. But the employee's duty has been done, the firm has been notified and there is an end to the matter.

Such a procedure is far too common. Consequently, many managers don't find out that they are presiding over an absence problem until it is far too late. What starts off as a simple hitch or hiccough frequently becomes a major issue. Once again, personnel managers are called in to preside over counselling interviews. The process becomes formalized. Trade union representatives sit in on meetings in order to ensure that no injustices take place, and frequently they're quite right to do so – since there is no evidence that anyone is managing the problem either fairly or consistently.

Of course, absence control procedures are vital, and disciplinary policy obviously plays a major part in them. But policies and procedures don't manage absenteeism. They safeguard the interests of both parties (employer and employee) in extreme cases. But extreme cases are the tip of the iceberg. The everyday cases that make up the bulk of the problem have to be tackled at source – and that means involving managers and making them specifically responsible.

Checklist

- Managers should be held responsible for keeping their own records
- They should be held responsible for the initial investigation and the initial discussion in every case, every time somebody is away from work. It is not a matter of running a major investigation or cross-examining individuals so much as finding out what actually happened and why. *That*'s their business
- Managers must be trained in basic counselling techniques. It is no good expecting them to cope with the sensitive issues of discussing delicate aspects of people's health or wellbeing if they have not had any help in how to do it. Yet it is very presumptuous to believe that only personnel managers have these innate skills, and that managers and supervisors (who, apart from being guardians of the company's goods and chattels, are often also fathers, mothers,

husbands and wives) have no potential aptitude in this direction

- Managers must be the trigger mechanism which ensures that higher levels (or outside specialist advice) are, eventually, involved in more complicated cases.

If these responsibilities are not made clear, it is very easy indeed to lose control. Opting out becomes a very simple process. Continuing illness (or continuing reasons for being apparently unwell) not investigated until it is far too late. As a consequence, the authority and status of managers is undermined and everybody suffers. Conversely, when managers *take* initiatives, absence problems are more readily solved and the role of management is, once more, underlined.

Of course, there are risks involved in delegating responsibility to managers. But it is very easy to minimize those risks by investing in some effective training and coaching (see Chapter 6) and, without question, the potential benefits are enormous.

Foremen, supervisors, section leaders and departmental heads really do know their employees very well indeed. They know about their personal lives, their friends, their interests, their family and their distractions. They know more about them than anybody else. Sometimes it is this very knowledge that encourages them to shy away from getting involved. Perhaps they suspect that they will simply confirm something that they think is there but would prefer not to have proved. They need encouragement and help. What nobody needs is to let them off the hook.

But it would be facile and simplistic to assume that managing absenteeism is simply a question of handing over the responsibility to managers and supervisors and then trying to forget about the problem.

In a major public utility, a newly appointed manager found himself confronted with a 25% absence rate. On asking personnel for 'help' he was simply implored by a demoralized officer to ensure he didn't upset the unions.

So he consulted the union representatives and established

the nature of the problem. He agreed that, initially at least, he wouldn't discipline anybody. With union understanding (i.e. neither agreement nor disagreement), he simply withheld weekend overtime from anybody who failed in the same week to report in on a Friday or a Monday.

Result No. 1: 19% immediate improvement in 3 weeks and a further 2% subsequently.

Result No. 2: Less overtime to more staff – instead of more to a few.

Result No. 3: Less overtime anyhow.

Result No. 4: There was a general change in the power structure. As the manager said, 'Someone has to be in charge – and it wasn't going to be them!'

Once an organization has decided to delegate responsibility in this way, the next stage is to explain the specific nature of the responsibilities involved in managing attendance. These are:

- explaining absence procedures
- keeping accurate records
- investigating and discussing every case
- establishing a clear plan of action
- asking for specialist advice in exceptional cases.

This brings us, of course, to the hoary old subject of job descriptions, better known as the crumpled piece of paper tucked away in the back of a manager's desk drawer or the neatly filed pristine copy kept in a loose-leaf folder somewhere in the personnel records department. Responsibilities for motivation, including managing attendance, need to be written into the objectives and job descriptions of managers and supervisors. Furthermore, they should be taken into account at the time when performance is reviewed, perhaps at the annual appraisal.

Personnel managers can do an enormously useful job in auditing management practice, and seeing that these kinds of responsibilities are being properly met. But they should not do managers' jobs for them.

Unless the circumstances are very exceptional, personnel specialists should not take any decision about an absentee. Instead, they should merely recommend action and provide help and advice. This may sound a little strong, especially in an IPM book, but it is one good way (and maybe the only way) of ensuring that the basic accountabilities are maintained. Remember, line managers do not necessarily fall over themselves to take on an even wider role. The historical reason why personnel managers were recruited in the first place was that many line managers opted out of the responsibility of managing people. Not a great deal has changed.

Explaining Attendance/Absence Procedures

How many employees actually understand what their employer specifically requires them to do when they need to be absent from work? The answer is probably very few indeed, because experience frequently indicates that when they are unable to come to work they get the procedure *wrong*.

In a well-known manufacturing company, everybody believes that if you cannot come to work, all you have to do is get your wife (or husband) to leave a message with the switchboard. The procedure actually says that you should personally telephone your boss and explain to him or her the reasons why you are unable to attend on that particular occasion. Some difference!

You can write down as many procedures as you like in as much detail as you want. You can publish them in works rules or employee handbooks. But you can't beat the well-tried process of requiring supervisors to explain what has to be done. And once that has been carried out, you only need to confirm it by publishing the correct procedure in simple English.

Absence, Sickness and Injury – Model Procedure

Notification of Absence

If you are absent for any reason (without the company's prior knowledge or permission), you must notify your supervisor as soon as possible on the first day of absence, explaining the reason for absence and its expected length. You should normally telephone yourself. However, if you are genuinely unable to do so, you can either arrange for someone to phone on your behalf with this information or arrange for someone to call in with a written note or message. The phone call or message should be made or arrive within one hour of your usual starting time, if possible.

Clarification of Absence

(a) If you are absent due to sickness for four or more days you must get a Self Certification Form from your doctor's surgery. You should complete, sign and send it in to your supervisor

(b) After seven calendar days' sickness, you must send in a doctor's certificate. (All sickness over seven days must be covered by a doctor's certificate.)

Failure to comply with the above notification and certification rules may affect your entitlement to Statutory Sick Pay.

Accidents or Injury at Work

If you have an accident or are injured on company premises or whilst working for the company off the premises, you must immediately report this to your supervisor/manager.

Medical Examination

The company reserves the right to require you to undergo a medical examination arranged and, if necessary, paid for by the company. You would be told of the results of such an examination.

Leaving Work Before the End of Normal Working Hours
You are required to seek your supervisor's/manager's permission if you need to leave work before the end of your normal working hours. Please give your supervisor/manager as much advance warning as possible of when and why you want leave and tell him or her when you go.

Note: The word 'supervisor' means the person who is responsible for the department or section in which you work.

Managing Attendance: A Manager's and Supervisor's Checklist

Timing
1. Keep up-to-date record cards and write down each absence promptly
2. Ensure that you talk to each absentee at the time he or she reports sick, even if it's on the telephone. Don't allow people to leave messages with the switchboard; if they've asked their wife or husband to phone, ask if you can speak to them personally, so that you can understand how bad they feel – and they can understand how much they'll be missed
3. See all absentees as soon as they return to work. Don't wait until they've been away on five or six occasions before you do anything.

Communication and Counselling
1. Tell them how much you missed them and how you managed to cope in their absence. Ask them to explain why they were away and what medical advice they took. If they didn't take any – why not? Is the problem likely to recur? And so on!
2. If you're not personally satisfied with the reason given for any absence, ask for advice, see the company doctor or nurse (if there is one), talk to your boss, but never say 'I don't believe you' unless you're sure. Sitting in judgement

is not part of the job. It may be part of someone else's job
– but not yours

3. Listen to the employee's comments and views. If
you're dealing with a case of repeated absence, discuss his
or her job, the working conditions or patterns. See whether
there's anything you can do to make life easier. Ask
employees what they are going to do to control the problem.
Point out the organization's basic requirements and standards for attendance

4. Always talk to employees in confidence and away from
the job

5. Listen – don't make up your mind beforehand. Ask
questions and wait for the answers

6. Take notes.

Representation

1. If there is a trade union, involve the elected representative. Tell him or her that you will be seeing all absentees
on their return to work. Tell the union what you'll be talking
about and ask its advice. If the procedure provides for union
reps to attend any such interviews, then invite them to
come; don't wait for them to find out

2. Don't take any disciplinary action without first informing the elected representative and listening to his or her
views.

Note Taking

Once you've established the reasons for absence and any
accompanying circumstantial information – write it down,
together with any other relevant facts, so that you know
what happened, when and why.

Establishing a Clear Plan of Action

Once you know the reasons for absence, it's much easier to
see the way towards a solution. However, whether the plan
is to see a doctor, talk to a senior manager, change working
hours or patterns, change shifts or jobs, or warn someone
as to their future behaviour, there are always three steps
you need to take:

1. Make sure the employee understands what action is to be taken, when and why. If disciplinary action is decided on, make sure it *is* taken. Issuing 'final' warnings that are not final simply undermines your authority
2. Make sure the action is, if possible, agreed with the employee, although if necessary you should take a unilateral decision
3. Make sure that a note of the action to be taken is entered in the employee's personal file.

Most counselling interviews will be much easier than anticipated. Not every employee is reticent – or reluctant to talk. Many of them will be only too pleased to meet you half way. But inevitably, sooner or later, a difficult case will be encountered.

The golden rule in such circumstances is to minimize what you say. You should explain the problem, maybe propose some options for solutions, but then be quiet and listen. If there's a lull in the conversation, don't fill it by launching into a statement. Let the employee speak! Prompt him or her by the use of words like 'Well?', 'So?' or 'And?' But don't answer your own questions.

The purpose of seeing someone about their absence is to establish the reasons for it, so that, if necessary, you can do something about it together. Absence counselling, like many other forms of communication, is a two-way street, so make sure that you and the employee exchange views and comments.

Asking for Specialist Help
Don't try to fight all your own battles! If you are confronted with a difficult case – perhaps a situation with no obvious solution, a family problem, an alcohol or drugs case, or a long-term sickness patient – take advice. The personnel department, your boss, your colleagues, occupational health specialists, GPs, social workers, councillors, priests – the list is endless – are all there to be asked. So ask them!

Finally, don't say you haven't the time. It's all part of the job: not to resolve problems with individuals is to under-

MOUNT PLEASANT LIBRARY
TEL. 051 207 3581 Ext. 3701

mine the team – and only teams and team efforts can overcome the hundred and one obstacles to success at work. It should come as no surprise that many of the world's most successful organizations can also boast some of the world's lowest absentee rates. Many of them delegate almost every aspect of 'people management' to the lowest level possible – with the proviso that advice and help should not only be made available, but should also be requested whenever they are needed.

Chapter 6
Training for Managing Attendance

Managers are not always enthusiastic about training programmes which purvey 'people' skills. Where they come from is a world in which people are a necessary but not often entirely welcome element. Managers themselves are not always selected or recruited because of their ability to lead, motivate or inspire others. Their qualifications are frequently different. Necessary, but different. Consequently they don't recognize in themselves those deficiencies for which others – training specialists and personnel managers – are only too keen to provide remedies.

Often their reaction is cynical, inclined to disbelief. Sometimes it may be politely curious – and in a minority of cases keen to accommodate or to learn. But the usual reaction is muted.

Wherever there is a lack of enthusiasm for developing people skills, you'll always find an accompanying deficiency – lack of ownership of the problem. One reason for this is that trainers all too rarely define the *problem* anyhow. They're very good at defining *symptoms*, but that's different. There is no point in sending managers away on a course in communication 'skills' unless they know why, how and when they are going to use them afterwards. There's no point in sending a manager away on any training programme just because his or her boss decided after the appraisal interview that they needed one! But that's all too frequently how it happens. For training to be of any use at all, recipients have to understand *why* they're receiving it. Understanding in this sense has to mean acceptance but not necessarily agreement.

On a seminar recently, the trainer was covering the usual round of introductions when he came to one delegate who said: 'I'm here because I've been told I've got to run team meetings.' The trainer asked him if he wanted to run such events. The reply 'No – but I've got to' was enough. Both parties knew exactly where they stood. The delegate knew and had accepted the reason for being on the course. Of course, there was still a long way to go, but at least the journey had a beginning and an end point.

Now consider the next delegate who simply said: 'I've just been told I've got to come.' What was he going to derive from the experience? And, incidentally, what was the trainer likely to derive from it either?

Training should help managers 'own' the problem of managing attendance. Here is an example of what can happen when this isn't the case.

During a meeting to discuss an endemic absenteeism problem in a commercial van manufacturers, a number of line managers all sat around blaming the unions, the pay structure, the shift system and the personnel department, roughly in that order. The personnel manager didn't help by not knowing any comparative absence rates between departments – and, even worse, by not being sure whether or not the problem was his responsibility. At the point when it was quite obvious that the meeting couldn't even decide who was accountable, it broke up. There was no point at all in discussing the remedies which those attending had assembled to hear!

The first step is to get managers to want to come. If you invite them, they won't necessarily respond. If you have them sent, they won't know why they're there. So what's left? The answer is simple enough. You have to persuade them with arguments which appeal to their instincts.

Let's go back for a minute to the working world in which many managers live. It's a world of budgets, projects, administrative issues, software, hardware, sales, marketing, research, development, engineering. But it's not a world of *people*, although obviously, it contains people.

Not all managers see people in the same way as personnel managers. In theory, they may understand that people are the conduit through which results are achieved. But, in their behaviour, many managers ignore this.

Conceptually, many managers know that employees need to be led, communicated with, consulted, recognized and so forth. Empirically, however, the same managers often drive, drag, ignore and undermine them. They may not realize that they're doing it – but, just the same, they are. And until they can understand, on the bottom line, where such attitudes lead, they're unlikely to change. So the first step in the persuasion process is to help them to understand the problem:

1. Tell them how to calculate absence rates
2. Go yourself, or send someone to sit with them and help them do it. If there are no records, help them set up a record-keeping system or do it with them for a few weeks
3. Tell them what the rates mean (e.g. 5% = 2 weeks per year for everyone, including them!)
4. *Then* – and only then – ask them if they think they have a problem.

Once the ownership is established, resist the temptation to jump in and provide instant solutions. There probably aren't any – and there's still another stage of regression to go through.

At this point, some managers still try to resist taking responsibility. This is not because they are lazy, ignorant, uncaring or disloyal. It's simply because they're being asked to step into an unfamiliar world. (I am assuming, incidentally, that if your managers are significantly different from the ones I am describing, you wouldn't be reading this book.)

The world into which you're taking them is a more sensitive place, one in which you have to talk to people about their private lives, their health, their operations – *personal* issues (the things they think that personnel managers should deal with, because that's their expertise). So it's not surprising that there's a regressive stage before any effective training can begin. Frequently this stage is heralded by an inclination to blame any of the following:

Unions
Discipline procedures
Poor selection by a predecessor
You.

Before you can introduce any training suggestions, it's necessary to help managers over this phase as well. Back to the persuasive arts, therefore, and follow this checklist:

1. Ask them how they would handle such problems as unions, discipline procedures etc.
2. Check to see how much they really know about these issues
3. Challenge any assertion that it's your problem and not theirs
4. Ask them what they want to do about it
5. Make them come up with their own action plan, *including a means or series of yardsticks by which they will measure their success*
6. If they won't listen to any of this – go and talk to their boss.

At this point you can design any training and support around the action plan which managers themselves have produced. Frequently there isn't a training problem anyhow and what is needed is a coaching programme in which you or your training manager work closely on an informal basis, to adapt, refine and adjust attendance action plans over a period of months. On the assumption that a series of training remedies may be required, here are a number of programmes which may be useful.

A. Full-day Training Course for Managers and Supervisors

Session 1: Introduction
Absenteeism is a sensitive subject: questioning employees about periods away from work can cause defensiveness – sometimes even aggression. However, someone has to do it – who should that someone be?

Quote some examples – from the organization, department or section. Explain current absence rates and what they mean.

Identify management's roles:

1. explaining attendance policies and procedures
2. keeping their own records
3. investigation and discussion
4. establishing jointly understood action, *which does not necessarily mean punishment*
5. seeking specialist advice in exceptional cases.

Session 2: Why People Stay Away From Work
Explain the basic causes of absence, underlining the experience of occupational health specialists.

Explain that not everyone is lazy – but some people are. Discuss the nature of jobs in your organization: in what areas is absenteeism more likely, for environmental, job or social reasons? Are other causes likely? List everything and discuss the possibility of minimizing such factors.

Session 3: Record Keeping
Emphasize the need for locally kept records and agree upon a basic format for ensuring this can be done. See the example in Chapter 4.

Session 4: Absence Policies and Procedures
Explain and answer questions about the organization's current policies and procedures for controlling attendance. Discuss any necessary amendments and alterations – and their possible implications for other agreements or terms and conditions of employment.

Session 5: Cures and Remedies
Ask the group for possible cures and remedies by quoting examples of current or recent cases and sharing your experience with theirs. Explain the link between absence control – through discipline procedures – and the law.

Examine each solution to ensure that what managers want to do is consistent with good company practice and not likely to cause an unnecessary employee relations incident.

Session 6: Counselling Skills
Where, when and how to raise the issue of absence with the individual: the use of questions; listening; note taking; jointly seeking solutions. Stress the need to be accountable – don't cop out, don't prejudge, don't condemn people to Draconian punishments. Look at the issue of evidence and how to use it.

Session 7: Case Studies
Managers look at some current examples of absenteeism within the organization and plan a counselling interview.

ACTION SESSION
Get each manager/supervisor to write down a specific commitment to future action.

Training Aids
You'll need a flipchart and some pens. Two films you might like to consider as support material are: *Gone Today – Here Tomorrow* (Guild Sound and Vision) and *Who's in Charge?* (Video Arts).

Suggested Ancillary/Support Training Activities
1. Role-playing exercises: get members of the course to act the roles of manager and absentee – and then to discuss what lessons they learned from the exercise
2. Challenge protestation with carefully prepared replies: 'We already do that' – 'Oh yes, when was the last time?', 'We tried it, but it didn't work' – 'Tell us about it and we'll see what you left out'; 'We haven't got time' – 'Well, tell me

something that's more important than getting your people to come to work.'
3. Issue handouts – but do limit the paperwork.
4. Within a few days *always* follow up action points with individuals personally.

B. Training for Employee Representatives

Session 1: Introduction
Introduce the subject by explaining that absence control is a sensitive subject, and one on which it is very easy for misunderstandings to occur. Explain that the session is about *controllable* absenteeism – or, put more positively, about *encouraging attendance*. Ask the representatives for examples from their own experience where individuals just do not come into work for 'human' reasons rather than because they are ill, although this adversely affects the company and other employees who have to cover for those absent.

Explain the objective of the session as an opportunity to air the matter, to review the extent of the problem in your organization and to show that managers and supervisors are able to handle individual cases in a non-disciplinary manner.

Session 2: The Nature of the Problem
Use examples and/or statistics you have from your own organization to illustrate the extent of the problem (use national figures also, if appropriate). Discuss how absenteeism affects bonus rates, productivity bonuses and job satisfaction. Using examples, indicate that absenteeism can add to stress on staff, lower morale generally and lead to friction in departments where everyone knows that people are not contributing as they should by being absent.

Ask the session to relate examples they have noticed (omitting names if they wish) of the organization not being able/willing to deal with the problem.

Session 3: Dealing with Absenteeism
1. Discuss with the session the techniques employed by the organization. Are they both fair and reasonable?
2. Ask how absence control could be improved. What do the representatives consider should be done? By whom? (Manager? Supervisors? Personnel specialists?)
3. Ask the session if they know the organization's absence-reporting procedures (make sure you do!). Ask

whether employees believe they have a right to 'sick' days
whether they understand self-certification
how procedures and policy could be made clearer.

4. Stress that the purpose of the company's/organization's policies on managing attendance is to *prevent* disciplinary action and to identify where illness or other factors are the real cause of absence, so that appropriate action can be taken.
5. Emphasize that the key issues are to assist individuals, to protect security of employment, to enable teams, sections and departments to be fully manned, and to show that dealing with the matter personally and informally at manager/supervisor level is usually better than going straight to a more formal level, away from the department.

Session 4: Conclusion
Thank representatives for attending. Ask them to discuss the messages of the session with managers or supervisors in their areas so that, wherever possible, joint initiatives can be taken.
Within a few days, follow up with each member of the session to find out what action has taken place.

Notes for Non-Specialist Trainers

People who are not themselves specialist trainers may have to organize and present training courses in absence control, especially in small companies and organizations.
These notes are designed to provide additional help, to

both line managers/supervisors and personnel specialists who may have to run such sessions.

Notes for Managers and Supervisors
1. Find out what the actual absence rates are for your own department or departments. If you don't know how to do this, and the figures aren't available, calculate them by:

dividing the total number of days' absence in any period by the total number of days available;
and then multiplying by 100 (see Chapter 4)

2. Find out whether absence is worse in any one department or section – or whether it's better! If you see any particular trends or indications, try to find out the reasons. Don't assume, for example, that absence is always worse at night, or in one particular kind of occupation
3. Look at the responsibilities for supervision. Are they clear? Are supervisors good communicators? Do they accept and practise their responsibilities for people?
4. Make sure you know the actual procedure for reporting absence, and the policy in your company for self-certification
5. If there's a company medical service, consult it and find out their experience. There may well be trends in absenteeism which you won't know about. For example, cases of individuals who are frequently off work around weekends or at times of peak work load
6. Don't assume that all absence is attributable to laziness or an uncaring attitude
7. Take a good look at working practices and methods. How much repetitive work exists? Are working conditions (i.e. environment, light, heat, etc.) worse than they should be? Is there any scope for making the work of your employees more satisfying?

Note for Personnel Specialists
1. Find out the dividing line between your responsibilities for absence control and those of line management and supervision

2. Remind yourself of the procedures for carrying out 'return to work' interviews

3. Examine the potential effect of all terms and conditions of employment upon attitudes to work. (Are your shift allowances up to date? What about wages?)

4. Look at absence rates and compare them from department to department and at different levels, so that you can direct your training effort at the right audience

5. Try to assess the reasons given for absence in order of the number of times they are put forward. How many instances of 'flu symptoms' are reported to you? Do they all come from the same sources? Are they more frequent in one department than another?

6. Find out how much management and supervisory training has taken place in 'people' skills

7. Ask yourself honestly whether the personnel function ever exercises responsibilities which should be borne by line management.

Chapter 7
Absenteeism and Trade Unions

It would be a mistake to assume that trade unions are, in some kind of perverse way, in favour of absenteeism and against the management of the problem. In fact, they are often highly critical of the way employers sometimes appear to abdicate their responsibilities. While they may mix up their role as responsible representatives with their anxiety to safeguard the interests of justice, they can, if treated in the right way, provide much more support for sensible absence control policies than many people believe.

In a local authority, which was under some pressure from local politicians to 'privatize' the garbage-disposal services because they were patently expensive and inefficient, the dustmen's shop stewards pointed out to management the damage done by absentees who were being allowed to 'get away with murder'! The reaction of management was incredulous – but the comment: 'You'd never back us up' was greeted by an even more devastating response: 'You've never asked us.'

Logic suggests that there is no earthly reason why shop stewards should wish to defend the indefensible. Sometimes this happens – but invariably it is only where organizations have allowed inexperienced representatives to go untrained or (rarely) where an individual is politically motivated and doesn't care too much about representation as a first priority.

Of course, unions are there to represent the interests of employees. But sometimes there is a real onus on the employer to explain what those duties are, and provide training facilities which will ensure that they are met.

Not many of today's trade unions are opposed to shop steward training, when it's provided by the company or organization. Certainly they want to be consulted on the nature and content of training programmes. They may even wish to meet with nominated trainers. But these are reasonable requests and it seems far better to accede to them and have well-qualified, responsible stewards to deal with on disciplinary issues than simply to sit around waiting for the unions to implement training themselves.

The initiatives are for employers to take; but provided training and help are made available, there is no reason at all to prevent them seeking the cooperation of trade unions in coming to terms with absentee problems.

Checklist for Personnel Managers

1. Ensure that all trade union representatives are properly accredited, have the organization's acceptance, and are trained to be competent in their duties. *This is a prerequisite to any initiative*

2. Ensure that trade union representatives know and understand the objectives of the business, including business plans and, wherever possible, budgets (and what they mean)

3. Ensure that representatives understand the basis for manning and staffing levels, together with the restrictions on overtime and the employment of casuals. Gain their acceptance for these decisions, if possible

4. Explain the absence problems and then specifically *ask* for support – or at least a dialogue

5. Agree a practical policy for handling all cases. Invariably such a policy will require (and why not?) the early consultation and involvement of representatives

6. Challenge specious opposition and, if necessary, seek the support of full-time officers in preventing it

7. Do not ask trade union representatives to do managers' jobs for them. It's not for shop stewards to communi-

cate the outcome of discussions or to justify what management has decided

8. Try to see shop stewards as a source of advice as well as (and maybe instead of) a source of opposition. This is pretty hard at times – if in doubt, refer to No. 1 in this checklist

9. Don't make the mistake of standing up for incompetent or prejudiced managers. If one of your colleagues has been an idiot, don't try to justify it

10. Ensure you're happy that representatives' facilities are adequate *and* being properly used

11. Tell your employees that management will always involve unions in such problems as absentee cases, so that you can build up trust from the bottom

12. Practice this participative approach on other company or organizational issues so that your behaviour towards trade unions is consistent and seen to be so

13. Explain what consistency in discipline means

14. Introduce the stewards/representatives to the company lawyer or doctor, wherever appropriate

15. Stay honest – be consistently straightforward and always categorically reject deceit.

In a rubber-manufacturing company, the full-time convenor called a walk-out without warning in support of his opposition to management's decision to discipline a poor timekeeper. This was contrary to all agreements between the company and the union, and the convenor concerned had just left a management–union meeting at which the issue had been a matter for discussion.

The response of the managing director was uncompromising: 'We're all entitled to one mistake in life, but you've just made two: breaking the procedure and lying to me. You and I are no longer in business together.'

Joint Management/Supervisor and Shop Steward Training

In recent years, a number of organizations have found that joint initiatives on training have paid major dividends in removing, perhaps forever, contentious issues which needed joint understanding. Absenteeism is one of them: many personnel managers are rueful about the number of occasions which they've had to preside over conversations at appeals along the lines of 'Oh no, I didn't' – 'Oh yes, you did.'

As we've observed before, most problems at work are about relationships. And since most bad relationships are the result of misunderstanding, it has to make sense, wherever trade unions are recognized, to consider joint management–union education and training programmes.

The following guidelines should prove helpful:

1. Ensure joint understanding of the agreement, procedures, dismissal policy etc.

2. Discuss jointly how environmental conditions can be improved

3. Ensure joint understanding of all 'the necessities' of the business: budgets, plans, unit wage costs etc.

4. Jointly explore practical attendance problems in both the short term and the long term

5. Ensure joint understanding of absence records and patterns

6. Establish joint understanding of the purpose of trade union facilities and particularly 'time off'.

Chapter 8
An Overall Strategy for Managing Attendance

Before applying any of the practical hints contained in this book, personnel specialists, managers and supervisors should ask themselves only two fundamental questions:

'Do I believe employees are basically lazy, that they'll opt out if they can, and that all they really need is good pay and close supervision?' and

'Do I believe that employees on the whole would rather work well than badly, would prefer to feel they are needed, and are rather demeaned by the suggestion that all an employer does is buy their time?'

If their answer to the first question is 'Yes', then clearly this book isn't for them. They'd be better off consulting Appendix 3 and brushing up on their knowledge of the law. They're going to need it.

If they answer 'Yes' to the second question, then they might start their new approach to managing attendance by establishing an overall strategy based on these principles:

- the provision of good physical working conditions, health and safety standards
- sound induction procedures to teach good practice
- small work groups always led by the same supervisors
- maximum job satisfaction
- clear delegation of responsibility to line management
- recognition that people often have good reasons for missing work and provision for such circumstances
- good management and supervisory training standards

- board-level responsibility for monitoring absence control
- a consistent approach which employee representatives and managers are fully aware of
- written policies for dealing with absence, including long-term sickness
- clear consistent discipline procedures with sensible time limits.

It's easy to see that employee commitment and attendance are inextricably linked. Naturally people will be away from time to time – but so much evidence suggesting that people who feel needed attend more than people who don't is difficult to ignore.

There are still many people in management whose initial instinct with an absentee is to ignore him or her until it becomes a problem; they only deal with him then because 'if I don't, they'll all be doing it'. So the initial instinct is negative, and this invariably gives rise to negative actions.

Warning people, threatening them, stopping their overtime, transferring them, even suspending or dismissing them, are all actions which may at some point in a manager's career have to be taken. But the motto '*pour encourager les autres*' is much better applied positively, in the belief that managing winners is easier than dealing with losers. And, at the end of the day, managing attendance is a great deal more fun than controlling absenteeism.

Chapter 9
Absenteeism and the Law

As you might imagine, judges have had a great deal to say about absenteeism and lateness – mainly because poor attenders frequently find themselves out of work. Of course, this is not necessarily their fault. But there does come a time when an employer says 'enough is enough' – and that's where the law comes in.

The best piece of advice this book could possibly offer on the subject of 'absenteeism and the law' is: don't try to be an amateur advocate! The problem is simple. Most law is based on precedent. Cases are being discussed constantly, before Employment Tribunals, the Employment Appeal Tribunal – even the House of Lords. Judge after judge can – and does – place his or her own interpretation on the meaning and intention of employment protection legislation on contracts of employment. It changes all the time.

So, all we're going to do in this chapter is set out some simple principles to follow. These will help you not to fall into the obvious traps. However, a second piece of advice is *get yourself a good solicitor* – preferably someone who specializes in employment law. If that presents a problem, ask IPM or ring one of the numbers in Appendix 8.

Simple General Principles

1. Definition of Absence
Anyone who fails to turn up on time at his/her *defined* place of work is *absent* and not entitled to pay, unless either they're genuinely sick and have notified the employer

according to the rules, or they have permission to be away, or there are genuine reasons for being away, which are outside the employee's control and acceptable to the employer. (It is worth noting that latecomers, by this definition, automatically count as absentees.)

2. Disciplinary Procedures
In Appendix 4 we have reproduced the report of a crucial test case, *Polkey v AE Dayton Services*. It is worth taking the trouble to *read it carefully*; note that the sense of it says that you *must* follow a fair discipline procedure. If you don't, any dismissal will almost certainly be adjudged unfair in a British tribunal, *even if it wouldn't have made any difference to the outcome of the decision.*

3. Find out the Reason Before Taking Action
Follow the ACAS Code of Practice (reproduced as Appendix 2). It might seem obvious, but you must make proper enquiries before you take any decision.

4. Dismissal for 'Genuine' Sickness is Permissable
Many employers think that absence through genuine (i.e. continuous, certified) illness is a cast-iron form of employment protection. 'Not so,' declared the Employment Appeal Tribunal in 1977. This view was confirmed three years later in another case which set out a number of conditions which govern the dismissal, for reasons of commercial necessity, of someone 'genuinely' sick:

  i. There has to be an investigation of the facts, the attendance record, reasons for absence and any patterns of absenteeism (e.g. lots of Mondays and Fridays, extensions of holidays etc.)
  ii. The employee must be consulted, given a chance to explain and shown the attendance record. (Try it sometime. You may be amazed at the number of people who simply *don't know* how bad the record is!)
  iii. The employee must be warned (under the discipline procedure) that the absence record is unacceptable, that

improvement is required within a given time limit *and what the consequences could be.*

As you will imagine, managing all this isn't easy. Each one of these steps is fraught with hazards, side issues and diversions. Family background, union reactions, the effect on team spirit/morale, the communication skills of managers (or otherwise), record keeping and administrative standards, all come into play as potential problems to be managed.

But it can be done. It *is* possible for an employer to say 'Enough is enough.' Employees can't hide forever behind the medical certificate (which is very difficult for a doctor to refuse). At the same time, the onus of responsibility is still on the employer to act fairly.

One way of doing this is to ensure that the maximum emphasis is placed on informal attendance management (i.e. the rest of this book!). Employers might think they're entitled simply to abide by the apparently plain provisions of employment protection legislation. But the more informal warning, counselling and discussion are the better. It's often a question of asking yourself whether you want to solve a problem – or punish the person you think is the cause of it!

5. Establish an Absence Control Policy Which Lays Down Clear Standards

A number of cases indicate that, where there is no formally agreed absence control policy, there's always a chance of inconsistency. If you lay down guidelines for everyone to follow, you can avoid

obvious unfairness
omissions
inconsistency
unnecessary time defending your actions in tribunal hearings.

Policy guidelines *do not* have to be based on an unacceptably high trigger point (i.e. the point or number of absences after which action will be taken). On the contrary, you should try to base the trigger point on the best records within the organization, not the average or the worst.

For example, you may find that one department can boast consistently *high* attendance – while another is consistently low. Don't take an average and don't negotiate the low standard as acceptable. Insist on the best, but emphasize that the process will be managed fairly and openly. And remember, whatever the trigger point, there's nothing to prevent informal discussion and investigation of *every* incident.

6. *Taking Medical Advice*
In long-term sickness cases, it is possible, with the employee's consent, to consult the organization or the employee's doctor. However, in doing so, you should:

- Tell the employee why you want their permission to do this (this is, effectively, mandatory)
- Get the organization's doctor to contact the employee's doctor
- Explain the nature of the job involved and why you are making the enquiry
- Ask for a medical report
- Consult the employee about the report and allow the employee to produce their own independent medical report if they wish to do so.

7. *Don't Simply Rely on Medical Certificates*
A number of cases confirm that medical certificates are not, on their own, a reliable or foolproof guide to taking action:

- The employee must be consulted about what the certificate(s) says
- The employer should not, without taking advice, draw his/her own conclusions.

8. *Consider Reasonable Alternatives Before Dismissing*
You don't have to create a special vacancy for someone who becomes unfit for the job for which they were originally employed. However, where an alternative opportunity

exists, don't simply assume that the employee wouldn't want it. Once again, to be on the safe side, *discuss it!*

Conclusions

Absence from work, in the final analysis, is caused by one of two factors:

CONDUCT – the employee doesn't WANT to come to work
CAPABILITY – the employee is PREVENTED from working by illness or injury.

Since you will have to make up your mind about the prime cause, it is unwise to confuse these two issues. Doing so invariably leads to trouble, inconvenience and cost. If, for example, an employee is persistently absent, it *may* be treated as a conduct issue and, if so, you should follow the fairly laid down guidelines for encouraging better conduct at work. As we have explained, these guidelines should provide for investigation, checking records, consultation/explanation and warning.

On the other hand, an employee *may* be genuinely prevented from working, by ill health. It *does* happen! Sometimes an employee will attend infrequently or sporadically because work has become too demanding. No sensible or humane employer would pretend that this was a disciplinary matter, yet at the same time the business has to carry on. Dismissal, at the end of the day, might be the only course available.

What should you do? Do you cite 'conduct'? Or do you go for 'capability'? (Now you can see why you should have a reliable legal advisor!) The answer lies in communication. Talk to the employee, find out what's causing the problem (if you can). Simple questioning should provide some hints about the kind of problem confronting you. Keep communicating. Consult the company doctor where there is one. Ask the employee for a medical report. Find out whether the employee's condition *does* prevent them from doing their job.

Only when you've exhausted the formal communication process can you make up your mind which course you're going to follow. If it's 'conduct', remember to invoke the provisions of your disciplinary code – or your absence control policy with which it conforms (and if it's to be any use, it must meet this standard). If it's a 'capability' problem you will need to carefully seek medical advice.

In either case, before dismissing anybody, you should consult a legal specialist. But whatever you do, *don't* dismiss someone for capability when what you really meant was conduct, or vice versa. You might have the best reasons in the world. But industrial tribunals are concerned with fairness – and the onus of proof is always on the employer to show that he or she acted fairly. Some conduct/capability issues are very clear, but if in any doubt ask a specialist!

Other Important Issues

Finally, here are a few more words of advice about important issues on which your organization should have a policy.

1. Pregnant Women

have a right to authorized absence with pay for time-off or ante-natal care as prescribed by their doctor. You cannot reasonably refuse such a request during working hours.

2. Health and Safety at Work (First Aid)

Health and safety legislation requires you to provide equipment facilities and training for first aid.

3. Sick Pay

Unless you expressly or implicitly provide otherwise, you have to pay full wages to any sick employee (unless you terminate the contract of employment during the period of sickness). While you are paying wages during illness, no deduction should be made for National Insurance Benefit received by the employee, unless the contract of employment provides for this.

4. Medical Advice

You should consider inserting a clause into the contract of employment enabling you to request that employees undergo a medical examination by a doctor of your choice at any time.

5. Your Company's Property

You should make it clear to employees that any property in their possession, when absent from work, must be looked after by them provided they are fit to do so. It would also make sense to ensure they know that, in the event of their being *unable* to care for your property, they should inform you.

6. Payment Following Dismissal Through Sickness

With certain exceptions and variations too complicated to list here (so take advice), wages must be paid to anyone dismissed whilst absent, sick, for the statutory period of notice due.

7. Aids

You should have a policy covering treatment of employees who contract AIDS. Dismissal where work is not affected is unfair.

8. Drugs, Drink, Disability etc

Different aspects of case law govern these three issues. There is no special protection for the disabled – but do take advice in the light of the individual circumstances. Alcoholism should be treated like long-term sickness, but drinking at work is clearly a 'conduct' issue. Drug taking is less clear than drinking – again, advice should be sought before any action is taken.

9. Cooperation with Medical Examination

If an employee refuses, without good cause, to give you permission to contact his/her doctor, you can consider dismissal without exhausting the procedure. However, you

MOUNT PLEASANT LIBRARY
TEL. 051 207 3581 Ext. 3701.

should seek an opinion first from your organization's doctor – or you could ask the employee to be examined by another doctor, if the contract of employment allows for this. *If the employee still refuses to co-operate*, it may be fair to dismiss – but, once again, do take advice, especially in the case of mental illness.

10. Epileptics

are required to disclose their condition *if they are at risk from their work*. They may be liable to dismissal if they are a risk to others.

Special Author's Note

As I have frequently confessed in this book, I'm not a lawyer. Nor are most of you. I make no apology for the fact that this chapter isn't a comprehensive guide to the law as it relates to absence. Nor is it an exhaustive analysis of the enormous number of cases which have built up over the past few years.

I hope it's a practical guide which will help you identify when to ask for advice. That's all it's meant to be. What I have set out is what I understand the law to provide for. For a good lawyer's interpretation, you should talk to a lawyer!

Chapter 10
The 'Return to Work' Interview

However good your motivation, however attractive the terms and conditions of employment, however cosy and comfortable the working environment, the fact is that sooner or later someone in your team is going to stay away from work. And when they eventually come back, somebody should see them, talk to them, tell them how much you missed them, and make them generally feel as loved and wanted as they no doubt are!

If you haven't carried out a 'return to work' interview before, here are a few hints which may prove helpful:

A. Preparation

You should be prepared for this brief encounter. You ought to know something about what you're going to say, to whom, and what kind of response you expect to get. So:

i. Did you miss them?
If you did – why? If you didn't – why not? Did you even know that they were missing? (Remember – everyone in your team should have a personal reason for being there)

ii. Why were they away?
What reason did they provide? When? Whom did they tell? (Was it you or someone else?) Who did the telling – the employee or their wife/husband/girlfriend? Do you think any of the traditional reasons for absence – besides the reason they gave – might apply?

iii. What's the home background?
Children, relations, parents, husband, wife, neighbourhood
etc

iv. What's the track record?
Is there any pattern of absenteeism? How many days off
have they taken this month/quarter/year? What reasons
were given for previous incidents?

v. Can anyone advise you?
Shop stewards, colleagues, former supervisors, company
nurse/doctor/safety officer/welfare officer/personnel etc

vi. How do you feel about the employee?
Are you able to be objective? Helpful? What kind of line
do you think you should take?

B.   Conducting the interview

 i. Since this is a potentially stressful situation, don't be
    surprised if you feel nervous. So may the employee.
    Be sensitive and courteous
 ii. Don't beat about the bush. Phoney conversations
     about last Saturday's football match or 'Did you have
     a nice weekend?' are not always very wise
 iii. Ask open-ended questions, i.e. questions that need
      answering with a bit more than 'Yes' or 'No.' For
      example, 'What does your doctor say' is better than
      'Have you seen your doctor?'
 iv. If you *know* the employee was playing truant, then say
     so and explain how you know. Don't coax him/her into
     further deceit!
 v. *Listen* – and improve your listening skills:

    look interested
    write down the answers to questions
    observe body language
    make eye contact
    eliminate all potential distractions

vi. Get the employee to talk with you. Remember, you're trying to solve a problem – not indicting someone for a crime
vii. If it gets heated/over-emotional, then *stop*. Allow time for recovery. If necessary, come back another day
viii. Don't accept answers at face value – probe
ix. Remember your manners. You are not being employed to abuse anyone. Abuse – however justified you think it is – will not count for you at subsequent appeals or tribunal hearings
x. If the first two or three questions, the first few minutes of the interview, indicate that you might be out of your depth, *stop* and seek help. As the saying goes, 'Make your excuses and leave'!
xi. Find joint solutions if you can – try to share the problem. Questions like 'What should *we* do about this?' bring more answers than 'Well, it's your problem, isn't it?' In finding solutions be prepared to exercise discretion on such issues as hours of work, timekeeping, duties, who works with whom etc (e.g. allowing somebody to come in half an hour late for a short period of time until they find a new childminder, making sure you explain to everyone affected by this what you have done and why)
xii. Close the interview by agreeing your action plan – whatever it is

C. Follow Up

i. Write up notes *promptly*
ii. Inform your boss, personnel manager and employee rep of what has been decided
iii. Send a copy to the employee (preferably *give* it to him)
iv. See him/her every week for a while
v. If it's a disciplinary matter, make sure you *have* followed the procedure, which includes informing the employee that it's a procedural issue.

Appendix 1
Twenty Do's and Don'ts for Managing Absence

1. **DO** your homework. Never hold a 'return to work' interview without consulting your records
2. **DO** keep your eyes and ears open. Being observant helps nip in the bud many an absence problem
3. **DON'T** give 'final' warnings that aren't final
4. **DON'T** do home visits unless everybody knows home visiting is part of the policy, and then only as a last resort
5. **DO** pay close attention to the working environment and working conditions
6. **DO** take advice from anyone who can throw light on a problem, particularly doctors and lawyers
7. **DON'T** approach a family doctor or any member of the social services without the employee's permission
8. **DON'T** be openly cynical or disbelieving, even if you know you're right
9. **DO** discuss each case of absence with the employee concerned
10. **DO** involve elected representatives early
11. **DON'T** lose your temper
12. **DON'T** run away from 'difficult' cases, e.g. absentee shop stewards or trade union activists
13. **DO** keep records and measure trends and patterns
14. **DO** monitor to ensure that any promised action is actually taken
15. **DON'T** be frightened of creating precedents, but
16. **DO** have a good reason for them and check them out with your boss
17. **DO** set time limits and dates for the completion of action plans

18. **DO** train and coach managers and supervisors in absence control

19. **DON'T** make the mistake of believing that it's only fair to treat everyone the same. Consistency is about always taking into account factors like age, sex, skill and aptitude, not about applying a standard of 'equal misery for all'

20. **DON'T** fudge the issue by pretending that a problem doesn't really exist, isn't as bad as it looks or will improve once the pay negotiations are over.

Appendix 2
The ACAS Checklist on Handling Absence from Work

This checklist, which is widely recognized as good management practice, is reproduced here with permission of ACAS.

This section considers how to handle problems of absence and gives guidance about short-term and long-term absences. A distinction should be made between absence on grounds of illness or injury and absence for reasons which may call for disciplinary action. Where disciplinary action is called for, the normal disciplinary procedure should be used. Where the employee is absent because of illness or injury the guidance in this section of the booklet should be followed.

Records showing lateness and the duration of and reasons for all spells of absence should be kept to help monitor absence levels. These enable management to check levels of absence or lateness so that problems can be spotted and addressed at an early stage.

How Should Frequent and Persistent Short-term Absence be Handled?

- Absences should be investigated promptly and the employee asked to give an explanation
- Where there is no medical advice to support frequent self-certified absences, the employee should be asked to consult a doctor to establish whether medical treatment is

necessary and whether the underlying reason for absence is work-related

- If after investigation it appears that there were no good reasons for the absences, the matter should be dealt with under the disciplinary procedure
- Where absences arise from temporary domestic problems, the employer in deciding appropriate action should consider whether an improvement in attendance is likely
- In all cases the employee should be told what improvement in attendance is expected and warned of the likely consequences if this does not happen
- If there is no improvement, the employee's age, length of service, performance, the likelihood of a change in attendance, the availability of suitable alternative work and the effect of past and future absences on the business should all be taken into account in deciding appropriate action.

It is essential that persistent absence is dealt with promptly, firmly and consistently in order to show both the employee concerned and other employees that absence is regarded as a serious matter and may result in dismissal. An examination of records will identify those employees who are regularly absent and may show an absence pattern. In such cases employers should make sufficient enquiries to determine whether the absence is because of genuine illness or for other reasons.

How Should Longer-term Absence through Ill-health be Handled?

- The employee should be contacted periodically and in turn should maintain regular contact with the employer
- The employee should be kept fully informed if employment is at risk
- The employee's GP should be asked when a return to work is expected and what type of work the employee will be capable of: the letter of enquiry approved by the British Medical Association may be used and the employee's permission to the enquiry should be attached to the letter

- On the basis of the GP's report the employer should consider whether alternative work is available
- The employer is not expected to create a special job for the employee concerned, nor to be a medical expert, but to take action on the basis of the medical evidence
- Where there is reasonable doubt about the nature of the illness or injury, the employee should be asked if he or she would agree to be examined by a doctor to be appointed by the company
- Where an employee refuses to co-operate in providing medical evidence or to undergo an independent medical examination, the employee should be told in writing that a decision will be taken on the basis of the information available and that it could result in dismissal
- Where the employee is allergic to a product used in the workplace, the employer should consider remedial action or a transfer to alternative work
- Where the employee's job can no longer be kept open and no suitable alternative work is available, the employee should be informed of the likelihood of dismissal
- Where dismissal action is taken, the employee should be given the period of notice to which he or she is entitled and informed of any right of appeal.

Where an employee has been on long-term sick absence and there is little likelihood of he or she becoming fit enough to return, it may be argued that the contract of employment has been terminated through 'frustration'.

However, the doctrine of frustration should not be relied upon since the courts are generally reluctant to apply it where a procedure exists for termination of the contract. It is therefore better for the employer to take dismissal action.

Where it is decided to dismiss an employee who has been on long-term sick absence, the normal conditions for giving notice will apply, even though in practice the employee will be unable to work the notice. In such circumstances, the employee should receive wages throughout the notice period or wages in lieu of notice as a lump sum.

Employees with Special Health Problems

Consideration should be given to introducing measures to help employees, regardless of status or seniority, who are suffering from alcohol or drug abuse. The aim should be to identify employees affected and encourage them to seek help and treatment. There are a number of symptoms related to alcohol or drug abuse including poor performance, changes in personality, irritability, slurred speech, impaired concentration and memory, deterioration in personal hygiene, anxiety and depression. Where it is established that an employee is suffering from alcohol or drug abuse, employers should consider whether it is appropriate to treat the problem as a medical rather than a disciplinary matter. In all cases the employee should be encouraged to seek appropriate medical assistance. In some areas there are specialist advice centres which can provide assistance.

Where an employee suffers from, or is thought to suffer from, a medical condition which makes him or her unacceptable to work colleagues, there may be workforce pressure to dismiss or threats of industrial action. Employers should bear in mind that they may have to justify to an industrial tribunal the reasonableness of any decision to dismiss. (DE and HSE have issued a booklet entitled *AIDS and employment* which explains that person-to-person transmission of the AIDS virus does not occur during normal work activities. There is no risk of becoming infected in most jobs and there are generally no grounds for dismissing or otherwise discriminating against an employee purely on the basis of infection or suspected infection.) Before any decision, the nature of the medical condition, working relationships, disruption to the business and the possibility of alternative work should all be considered.

Failure to Return from Extended Leave on the Agreed Date

Employers may have policies which allow employees extended leave of absence without pay, for example to visit relatives in their countries of origin or relatives who have emigrated to other countries, or to nurse a sick relative. There is no general statutory right to such leave without pay and whether it is granted is a matter for agreement between employers and their employees or, where appropriate, their trade unions.

Where a policy on extended leave is in operation, the following points should be borne in mind:

• The policy should apply to all employees, irrespective of their sex, marital status and racial group

• Any conditions attached to the granting of extended leave should be carefully explained to the employee and the employee's signature should be obtained as an acknowledgement that he or she understands and accepts them

• If an employee fails to return on the agreed date this should be treated as any other failure to abide by the rules and the circumstances should be investigated in the normal way as fully as possible

• Care should be taken to ensure that foreign medical certificates are not treated in a discriminatory way: employees can fall ill while abroad just as they can fall ill while in this country

• Before deciding to dismiss an employee who overstays leave, the employee's age, length of service, reliability record and any explanation given should all be taken into account.

An agreement that an employee should return to work on a particular date will not prevent a complaint of unfair dismissal to an industrial tribunal if an employee is dismissed for failing to return as agreed (s140 of the Employment Protection [Consolidation] Act 1978). In such cases all the factors mentioned above and the need to act reasonably should be borne in mind before any dismissal action is taken.

Appendix 3
More Medical and Legal Issues

As I said earlier, this isn't a book about how to deal with long-term or chronic illness. Nor is it a book about the law. Hopefully, it is instead a source of practical advice; if you take it, it may help avoid unnecessary complications. Here, therefore, are a few hints about the use of medical and legal advice:

1. If there isn't a company doctor, get one, *and use him or her as a doctor!* In other words, ask only for advice on the employee's capability for work. Doctors are in business only to advise on medical conditions
2. If an absentee's conduct is unacceptable, don't dismiss or discipline him or her on grounds of capability

If someone is away for 6 months with a bad toe, question his or her capability, *i.e. capacity for work. But don't sack him for lying. The first is easy to establish. The second is almost impossible.*

3. The law relating to 'conduct' is virtually all based on precedent, i.e. case law. Without expert guidance, it's a minefield. Get yourself a decent company lawyer who understands employment law (IPM can supply advice on both medical and legal sources.)
4. Don't ever dismiss anyone on medical grounds without taking medical advice. There is a clearly established obligation on employers to do this
5. Don't ask doctors or lawyers to take your decisions for you. They shouldn't do it and invariably won't
6. Don't be misled into believing that doctors' notes are

a complete justification for inaction on your part. There is nothing to prevent you from taking steps to have an absentee medically examined (provided that the employee consents). Remember that statutory requirements oblige employers to obtain the employee's consent where information is required from the absentee's own GP

7. If you can't obtain the employee's consent to medical examination, see your own company lawyer before taking any further action

8. If you do seek medical advice, get it in writing, and ensure that it covers the employee's current condition, the extent to which it may change and the alternative employment the employee may be likely to be able to undertake

9. Ensure the employee is also given the opportunity to obtain a medical report

10. You must consult an employee before dismissal on the grounds of ill health

11. Don't make the mistake of assuming that, because you're a small company, there's no duty to take medical advice on ill-health cases.

Appendix 4
The House of Lords Decision on
Polkey v A E Dayton Services Ltd

This case-law decision in 1987 by the House of Lords has enormous implications for every employer, so the review of the case published in Industrial Relations Review *and* Report *on 15 December 1987 is reproduced in full here. I am grateful to the editor for granting me permission to reprint it.*

The case establishes that industrial tribunals should always, regardless of other considerations, consider whether an employer has acted reasonably, in the light of their knowledge at the time, in dismissing *without warning or consultation: 'It is what the employer* did *that should be judged – not what he might have done.'*

It's no longer possible for an employer to excuse a procedural failure by pleading that it wouldn't have made any difference to the outcome. Employers are expected to follow procedures both in 'capability' and 'conduct' cases. The clear implication is that invariably *you are expected to consult, warn – and act reasonably, with regard to fairness and the wellbeing of the individual.*

Elsewhere in this book we have pointed out that the law on dismissal is not by any means easy. As a simple maxim, stick to the procedures, warn people about their conduct, discuss capability issues, and always consult before you dismiss anyone.

Sticking to such principles need not make any difference to your rights to manage – but not doing so could be very damaging indeed. And, if in doubt, take specialist advice.

Lords Overrule *Labour Pump*

The House of Lords has overruled *British Labour Pump Ltd v Byrne* and the various other authorities supporting the 'any difference' test. Their decision in *Polkey v A E Dayton Services Ltd* restores the importance of following fair procedures before dismissing and is likely to have a significant impact on the approach taken by industrial tribunals in the future.

On 27.8.82 Mr Polkey was told 'quite out of the blue' that he was redundant and was sent home that same day. The industrial tribunal hearing his unfair dismissal complaint described the manner of his dismissal as 'a heartless disregard of the provisions of the code of practice'. In particular, it referred to para. 46 of the code of practice issued under the Industrial Relations Act 1971, which emphasizes the need for warning and consultation before a dismissal for redundancy.

With reluctance, however, it felt bound to find the dismissal fair because, if the code of practice had been followed, he would still have been dismissed: the failure to warn or consult made no difference. This decision was upheld by the EAT and Court of Appeal.

More than five years after his dismissal, the case eventually reached the House of Lords. The sole question before it was whether the industrial tribunal had been entitled to apply the 'any difference' rule.

The House of Lords stated emphatically that it was not so entitled. S.57(3) of the EP(C)A states that, once the employer has established a reason for dismissal, the fairness of the dismissal shall depend on whether the employer acted reasonably in treating that reason as sufficient for a dismissal. As the House of Lords had explained in *Devis & Sons Ltd v Atkins*, the reasonableness of the employers' actions is to be judged in the light of their knowledge at the time of dismissal. It is thus not permissible, their Lordships said in *Polkey*, to take into account the fact that, with hindsight, the defect in procedure could be shown to have made no difference. There is no scope, said Lord Mackay of Clashfern, 'for the tribunal considering whether, if the employer had acted differently, he might have dismissed the employee. It is what the employer did that is to be judged, not what he might have done.' On the other hand, he said, 'If the employer could reasonably have concluded in the light of the circumstances known to him at the time of dismissal that consultation or warning would be utterly useless he might well act reasonably even if he did not observe the provisions of the code.' He cited with approval a passage from the EAT's decision in *Sillifant v Powell Duffryn Timber Ltd*, where, having stated that in general a procedural failure may lead to a finding of unfairness, the EAT recognized that 'there may be cases where the offence is so heinous and the facts so manifestly clear that a reasonable employer could, on the facts known to him at the time of dismissal, take the view that whatever explanation the employee advanced, it would make no difference.'

In this case, the industrial tribunal should not therefore have considered what would have happened if the employer had consulted. It should simply have asked whether they acted reasonably, in the light of their knowledge at the time, in dismissing without warning or consultation.

Review of Authorities

The House of Lords then examined the various authorities on the question of how the fairness of the procedure leading to a dismissal affects the fairness of that dismissal. Two early cases, *Earl v Slater & Wheeler (Airlyne) Ltd* and *Vokes Ltd v Bear*, emphasized the importance of following a fair procedure. In *Earl*, the National Industrial Relations Court (NIRC) gave the example of an accountant dismissed for suspected embezzlement when there were in fact no grounds for such suspicion. Such a dismissal would be unfair, the NIRC said, even if the accountant was later proved guilty. These cases were approved by the House of Lords in *Devis* and again in *Polkey*.

The cases followed by the industrial tribunal in this case all came later. The 'any difference' rule is attributed to the EAT in *British Labour Pump Co Ltd v Byrne*, though it had been introduced in a number of earlier cases. In *British Labour Pump*, a dismissal for suspected dishonesty was found unfair because the employers had not carried out a proper enquiry. The EAT said that the correct approach in such cases is to ask two questions: first, have the employers shown on the balance of probabilities that they would have taken the same course had they held an enquiry?; secondly, have the employers shown that, in the light of the information which they would have had had they held a proper enquiry, would they still have acted reasonably in dismissing?

This 'any difference' principle was vigorously attacked by the EAT in *Sillifant v Powell Duffryn Timber Ltd*, on much the same grounds as the House of Lords in *Polkey*. It confused justice to the employee with the reasonableness of the employers and required the tribunal to take into account matters not known to the employers at the time of dismissal. However, *British Labour Pump* had by that time been approved by the Court of Appeal in *W & J Wass Ltd v Binns*, and the EAT in *Sillifant* felt bound therefore to apply the 'any difference' test.

The EAT's arguments in *Sillifant* were considered by the Court of Appeal in *Polkey*, but the court held that *Wass v Binns* was binding authority which the industrial tribunal and EAT had been right to follow. The court justified the 'any difference' test by saying that the gravity of the failure to observe a proper procedure, which was clearly relevant to the question of fairness, could be measured by its effect in practice. 'Thus . . . there may be cases where the evidence of misconduct is not so clear as to justify instant dismissal and which *could* be capable of explanation, but where, on examination, the employee has no explanation to put forward. In such a case, the failure to seek an explanation from the employee, which fairness would in principle require, will not make any difference.' Their Lordships disagreed. Measuring the gravity of the procedural default in terms of its effect required an examination of matters other than the employers' conduct, which could not have been known to the employers at the time of dismissal. Accordingly, *British Labour Pump, Wass v Binns* and the other cases supporting the 'any difference' test were all overruled.

Guidelines for a Fair Dismissal
By overruling the *British Labour Pump* test, their Lordships made it clear that it is no longer open to employers to excuse a procedural failure by establishing that in fact it made no difference to the outcome. However, their Lordships went even further in emphasizing the importance of following fair procedures. Lord Bridge of Harwich stated that 'in the great majority of cases' employers will not be regarded as having acted reasonably if they have not taken such procedural steps as are necessary, in the particular circumstances, to justify the dismissal. 'Thus,' he continued, 'in the case of incapacity, the employer will normally not act reasonably unless he gives the employee fair warning and an opportunity to mend his ways and show that he can do the job; in the case of misconduct, the employer will normally not act reasonably unless he investigates the complaint of misconduct fully and fairly and hears whatever the employee wishes to say in his defence or in explanation or mitigation; in the case of redundancy, the employer will normally not act reasonably unless he warns and consults any employees affected or their representative, adopts a fair basis on which to select for redundancy and takes such steps as may be reasonable to avoid or minimize redundancy by redeployment within his own organization.'

Relevance of 'Any Difference' Test to Remedies
The House of Lords accepted that the fact that the employee would have been dismissed even if a proper procedure had been followed, though irrelevant to fairness, might be relevant when determining the remedy. Thus in cases of misconduct, if it is shown that, though the employer had not investigated the matter adequately, the employee was nevertheless guilty, then compensation may be reduced under s 73(7B) (the basic award) and s 74(1) and (6) (the compensatory award). Similarly, in cases of redundancy, if the tribunal concludes that, on the balance of probabilities,

the employee would have been dismissed even if a fair procedure had been adopted, then compensation may be reduced to reflect the probability that dismissal would have resulted in any event.

As Lord Bridge pointed out, this does not mean that a finding of unfair dismissal would be of no benefit to the employee in such circumstances, because the employee would still probably be entitled to some compensation. Another reason he gave was that the industrial tribunal must, after making a finding of unfair dismissal and before considering compensation, decide whether to order reinstatement or re-engagement. In most cases of redundancy or misconduct tribunals would be likely to find that such an order would be impracticable, but this is not necessarily so, since the employers' circumstances might have altered by the time of the tribunal hearing; for example, in redundancy cases new vacancies might have arisen.

Appendix 5
Using Joint Consultative Machinery

A number of companies consciously employ joint consultative machinery to support their attendance policies. Roles have to be carefully defined and, as a prerequisite, management–union relationships have to be positive and well managed. The usual steps are along these lines:

1. The employee's consent is sought for his or her record to be discussed
2. He/she is invited to attend
3. The facts are put to the JCC and clarification sought on points of detail
4. The JCC is invited to recommend any action that might be taken. This may cover support and help in cases of personal difficulty, advice both to employee and manager or disciplinary action
5. It is not good practice in these cases to delegate the responsibility for action to joint bodies. To do so places employee representatives in an invidious position
6. Recommendations and the decisions that follow are minuted and may be published subject to the chairman's (management's) discretion.

It is vital, if you're considering this line of approach, to avoid 'kangaroo courts'. By all means use consultative machinery – but do bear in mind that it *is* consultative in its nature. In other words, the JCC should be used for an exchange of views between management and employees or their representatives prior to *management* decision.

Appendix 6
Example of Company Practice

This example is taken from the petrochemical industry. The current absence rate is 1½–2%.

1. All attendance is recorded by first-line supervisors and notified each week to the Employee Relations Manager
2. All absentees are seen by their immediate (first-line) supervisor on their return to work
3. Anyone who is absent for 2 days or more is visited at home by the nurse or by the immediate supervisor
4. Any certificated medical condition is discussed between the employee and the nurse on the return to work, and a note sent to both the supervisor and departmental head, advising them on any implications
5. Any employee who is unable to come to work *must* personally speak to his or her immediate supervisor or line manager or, if he is too ill, must get someone else to do it for him
6. Anyone who doesn't report in without notification is automatically visited
7. The emphasis throughout the entire procedure is on '*care*'. The company cares about its employees. We care for them – and their families. If there are problems, it wants to know about them.

Great emphasis is placed upon positive management – well trained supervision, clear objectives, good communications. Disciplinary action is rare and labour turnover very negligible. The Employee Relations Manager is specifically not required to take any part in the absence control process

unless disciplinary action is involved. The company nego-
tiates with three unions, TGWU, AUEW and EEPTU.

Appendix 7
Procedures for Controlling Absence at Tesco

The following extracts from Tesco's policy are reproduced here with the permission of the Company. They come from a far bigger and more comprehensive document which was prepared by the Company's personnel department. It is reproduced here, not because Tesco pretends to have solved the problem of absenteeism, but because it is a good example from an industry which has traditionally suffered from endemic problems of high labour turnover – and poor attendance. Tesco testifies that this policy is measurably and positively influencing attendance patterns.

Purpose

Excessive absenteeism seriously affects the Company's overall profitability and productivity. Although some absence is outside management's control, levels of absence can be reduced by the implementation of positive policies and procedures. An overall and consistent approach to absence is essential with the aim of minimizing disruption caused by absenteeism, while at the same time treating employees fairly and compassionately.

In order to satisfy the Company's objectives in controlling absence, it is recognized that the following conditions must exist:

- Rules concerning absence must be clearly communicated, to be understood by all employees. Equally, management involved in enforcing the rules must act uniformly in applying the basic controls

- In order to monitor absence, specific records must be kept for each employee, which must show the duration of and reasons for all spells of absence
- Management must conduct a sufficient enquiry with regard to each spell of absence, as proper investigation and consultation with each employee is essential
- Before taking any disciplinary action, management should ask themselves whether they have considered all available options and must be mindful of the need to act reasonably in all circumstances
- In dealing with absence, a clear distinction must be drawn between absence on the grounds of genuine sickness and absence for other reasons, as different courses of action are appropriate in each case.

Dealing effectively with absence calls for a continuous and co-ordinated effort by line management, including supervisors. Employees and their representatives will want to see management showing an understanding towards those who need to be genuinely absent, and taking appropriate action against any who abuse the system at the expense of their colleagues. Within the framework of these procedures line management will be expected to play a key role in influencing employee behaviour and performance and creating a purposeful working atmosphere which plays a large part in reducing absence.

Absence Procedures

1.0 Overall Considerations
In the main, the Company procedures relate to the specific actions which must be taken when absence occurs. There are, however, general considerations which must be taken into account when seeking to control absence.

1.1 Pre-Employment Interview – Applicant Screening
During the pre-employment interview, an in-depth inquiry into the job applicant's prior attendance and work habits

should be made. Stress the importance that our Company places on good attendance and overall dependability, so that the applicant is aware even at this early stage of the importance that the Company places in this area.

1.2 Induction
Ensure that the employee is made totally aware and understands the rules and procedures for absence. Emphasize from the outset that avoidable absenteeism and tardiness will not be tolerated. Point out the high cost of non-attendance in terms of disrupting work schedules, inefficiency, drop in productivity, work pressures that are placed on colleagues, overtime payments and the drop in quality of customer service. Ensure that each employee understands that a specific record of their attendance will be kept and that the duration of absence and the reasons will be kept within their personal file.

1.3 Probationary Period
Any tendency towards absenteeism and lateness must be watched carefully during this period. Specific instances should immediately be brought to the employee's attention and the Company's stance on avoidable absenteeism re-emphasized. If a problem is materializing, then ensure that the matter is also approached formally at the relevant review stages within the probationary period. Take careful note of any reference responses received during this time which indicate absence or lateness problems with previous employers or from school records. If the employee is exhibiting the same traits with our Company, then it is likely to be a continuing problem. Most importantly, re-check that the rules on absence have been clearly understood.

1.4 Constant Application of the Absence Rules
Ensure that employees are made to follow every aspect of the rules, as one lapse can lead to inconsistency and an apparent laxity of approach. Ensure that a statement of absence form is completed on *every* occasion; that the employee is properly interviewed and the reasons for

MOUNT PLEASANT LIBRARY
TEL. 051 207 3581 Ext. 3701.

absence examined in depth; that their individual record of absence is filled in in front of them and is highly visible. This ensures that the healthy stay-aways don't get away with absence and that the weekend and holiday stretchers know that the management are wise to their pattern.

1.5 Publicize and Praise Good Attendance

Place monthly results of department and overall store performance on the staff noticeboard so that everyone knows the situation. Where Departments are performing well, ensure that the Department Head makes this known to staff and that the Manager/Staff Manager also mentions the fact when walking round the department. Individual records of good attendance over a 6-month/yearly period should be singled out for praise by line management.

1.6 Supervision and Counselling

A disciplined attitude toward unexcused absenteeism and tight control must be exercised by all members of management. Where appropriate, and justifiable, quick and decisive disciplinary action should be taken with continuous offenders, where counselling fails to correct the problem. However, this is not just a one-way exercise. Each line manager will be expected to examine his/her philosophy and management style and to learn more about why an employee avoids coming to work. It is generally accepted that most employees will come to work when able, if someone at work cares enough that they come. Establishing the proper climate and working environment is essential.

1.7

Having established the rules, procedures and documentation to assist with absence control, then it is encumbent upon Management to ensure that they are consistently applied in their entirety. To ensure that this occurs, absence control will be considered a measure of performance in judging the overall effectiveness of line Management and Supervisors. In addition, audits of Personnel policies, practices and procedures within stores will specifically include a detailed investigation of this area.

2.0 Rules Relating to Absence from Work

[Tesco lists a comprehensive set of rules which are not reproduced here.]

3.0 Documentation to Accompany Absence Procedures

3.1.2 Initial Notification

3.1.3 Statement of Absence

3.2 Individual Record of Absence
The main purpose of this form is to maintain a graphical individual record of the employee's absence record (see page 110 below). It must be completed at the time of certification interview in order that it is highly visible and so that the employee sees that their performance is being monitored. It will illustrate patterns of absence, recurring health problems, total hours lost and number of times absent/late. It can also be used to make comparisons with dept./store absence rates, assist with determining the effect of any action taken and support decisions resulting in discipline, dismissal, demotion or promotion.

4.0 Differentiating Different Types of Absence

4.1 All forms of absence, with the exception of holidays and extended leave, have to be supported by a Statement of Absence Form and recorded on the employee's individual record of absence.
4.2 It is, however, important to clearly differentiate and

define specific types of absence, particularly when considering the payment considerations applicable to each category:

Absence Due to Sickness
Unauthorized Absence – Unpaid
Authorized Absence – Paid
Authorized Absence – Unpaid

5.0 The Decision to Pay or Not

5.1 Payment is only due when genuine sickness takes place or Management has agreed payment in advance for an authorized absence, e.g. bereavement leave. There are no fixed 'golden' rules which determine whether or not payment should be made, as this is purely a Management decision based upon the reasons contained within the Statement of Absence form and the outcome of the interview with the employee upon returning from absence. It is an integral part of the Company's policy that any such decisions made by Management are fair, reasonable, supported by facts and consistent.

5.2 The key elements in assisting Management to come to a fair and reasonable decision are dependent upon the following factors:
[there follows a detailed and well-described list of circumstances].

6.0 Disciplinary Action Relating to Sickness and Absence

6.1 There may be circumstances arising from the procedures where some form of disciplinary action may be appropriate. No specific guidance can be given as to what action to take, or indeed when to take it, as each case will be different dependent upon the facts. The following situations would normally be ones where consideration must be given to instituting the disciplinary procedure:

- Failure to follow the notification rules by not contacting the store during the first day of absence and having no good reason for doing so
- Providing a totally unsatisfactory reason for being absent from work, e.g. taking the day off to go to a football match
- A continuing pattern of unauthorized absences
- Deliberate falsification of the Statement of Absence Form.

The last example, above, is potentially a very serious act of misconduct, as indeed the Statement of Absence Form contains a specific warning that any false statement may result in summary dismissal.

6.2 The most difficult cases to deal with relate to patterns of intermittent absence due to sickness which at face value appear to be genuine and, in some cases, are supported by Doctor's statements. Management should not feel that, just because the sickness does appear genuine, no action can be taken. If a pattern of absence does develop which is due to genuine sickness, then the most appropriate method of dealing with the situation is to warn the employee about the reliability of their attendance.

6.3 If the complaint is one of reliability, then there is no question of arguing over the authenticity of sickness. All the absences may be genuine, but when collated together they show a bad attendance record which shows the employee as being unreliable and disciplinary action can be taken on this basis. By using this strategy employees do not feel that the authenticity of their sickness is being challenged but are made to understand that the needs of the business demand that employees are reliable and are regularly available for work. Persistent illness, whilst genuine, gives rise to a disruption of the store's day-to-day operations.

6.4 Management contemplating disciplinary action for reliability must observe certain basic ground rules, which are:

- Clearly establish the facts: Is the absence record significantly worse than that of others? Is there a pronounced pattern of absence (e.g. every Saturday or when school holidays occur)? Do not include periods of hospitalization which have sorted out a medical problem and have contributed towards improved attendance

• During the interview, fully discuss the absence record – show the employee the record of absence form, because it will graphically illustrate the amount of absence and bring home the facts

• Probe to see if there are problems at home or work and discuss whether a change of job will provide a solution

• Examine the reasons for the absence carefully and, if there is an underlying health problem, try to persuade the employee to see the Doctor, both for their own welfare and in view of the consequences to their continued employment if the situation persists

• Explain what is considered to be a reasonable standard of attendance, based upon what is being achieved by other members of staff

• Set a reasonable period over which the attendance record will be reviewed and explain the consequences if an improvement is not achieved. This should obviously be linked to the warning issued.

7.0 Long-Term Sickness

7.1 One of the most difficult problems experienced by Management is that where an employee is absent for a very long period of time due to ill health.

7.2 How long you can wait before taking action will depend on many factors, e.g. the importance of the employee's job; the difficulty in continuing with a temporary replacement; the likelihood of the employee ever returning to work in the foreseeable future; the employee's length of service etc. It is normally safe to wait before doing anything until the employee's sickness entitlement is exhausted.

7.3 The main factor, however, is the Company's need for the job to be done. Without becoming unsympathetic in the situation, there must come a time where the Company's need to run the business efficiently overrides the need to provide long-term security of employment for the employee.

If an employee has been absent for 6 weeks, then contact your Regional Personnel Office and make them fully aware of all the circumstances.

7.4 The Personnel Department will then decide upon the best method of contacting the employee on a more formal basis, i.e. a letter or a personal visit. The Personnel Officer will try to ascertain an expected date of return, but if this is unavailable or appears to be unreasonable, then the employee's permission will be obtained to write to their Doctor.

7.5 This next step is vitally important, as any future decisions can only be based on current information about the true position. The purpose of the Doctor's report is not to obtain a detailed diagnosis but to enquire about the nature of the illness, how soon the employee will be fit to work again, what future treatment is envisaged and, when the employee is fit to return, whether it will be in a full capacity or it will necessitate light duties for a period of time or completely alternative work. The Doctor is given full information concerning the employee's job and working conditions, in order that the opinion is given in the correct context. The Company does, of course, bear any charge which the Doctor makes for giving this statement.

7.6 Upon receiving this information the Personnel Department will normally be in a position to assist Management in making a decision. However, if the report fails to give the correct information or is considered inadequate, then the employee may be asked to attend a Company medical.

7.7 Having obtained the true medical position, the Company would then have one of two options:

• The date of return is reasonable and the Company will wait for the employee to return, with the proviso that if the employee does not return by the stated date, then the Company will review the situation again; or

- The date of return is unreasonable or cannot be predicted, in which case a meeting will have to take place with the employee to fully discuss the situation.

7.8 The employee must be aware that any discussions will take place in the context of a possible dismissal due to their long-term ill health, and an employee representative will be allowed to be present if required.

7.9 If the second option has to be chosen then, before discussing the situation with the employee, the following circumstances must be taken into account in assessing the situation:

- Is the employee about to undergo further treatment which could radically change the situation quite quickly?
- The nature, length and effect of the employee's incapacity
- The employee's previous and likely future service with the Company
- The importance of the job and the need for a permanent replacement
- The availability of alternative employment, should this be applicable in the light of the medical report, either at the base store or another store in the surrounding area. However, the Company is not obliged to create a job. A vacancy can only be offered if a vacancy exists.

7.10 The circumstances should then be fully discussed with the employee, but remember this is not a one-way discussion. The Company must fully consider the employee's views before coming to a decision.

7.11 Having taken all the circumstances into account, and if no alternative work can be found or considered, then one of two options is available:

a) If the date of return is considered unreasonable, then a deadline can be set (if applicable), after which time, if the employee has not returned, he/she will be dismissed contractually; or

b) If there is no question of the employee being fit for some time or if he/she will never be fit to carry out their duties again, then the employee can be given contractual notice of dismissal.

The preceding guidelines outline the Company's Policy in such cases and a failure to follow a fair procedure will inevitably render any dismissal unfair.

Record of Absence

	YEAR:
NAME:	NORMAL WORK
	PATTERN:
DEPT:	S M T W T F S

W/C S M T W T F S	REASON	ACTION	TOTAL A	TOTAL S	TOTAL U	POSS HRS	TOTAL ABS.

S = SICKNESS
A = AUTHORIZED ABSENCE
U = UNAUTHORIZED ABSENCE

Standard letter sent to individuals who are away from work

RE: ABSENCE

Dear

I was sorry to receive word that you are not able to attend work and particularly that you anticipate not being able to come into work before the end of a week. As you know, I am unable to arrange any payment which may be due to you without a satisfactorily completed Statement of Absence and I am, therefore, enclosing the Statement for completion. It is essential that I receive this within a week of your first day of absence.

When you fill in the Statement, if there is any information that you do not know, please state this, although a form lacking in important details will affect your benefit. Please remember that a Statement of Absence must be completed even if you have no benefits due. Please be specific about the reason for absence. A vague statement such as 'unwell' cannot be accepted. If your absence should continue for more than 3 days, you must keep me informed of the results of your visits to the doctor.

I will see you on your return and hope you are able to return soon.

Yours sincerely

on behalf of
TESCO STORES LTD

Statement of Absence

SURNAME _____ INITIALS _____ BRANCH NO. _____ MAN NO. _____

INITIAL NOTIFICATION

Date and time of notification: _____

How has the absence been notified (personal visit/telephone/other) please specify _____

By whom has the absence been notified (employee/other) please specify _____

The reason given for the absence is _____

Is employee able to visit premises to complete statement below? Yes/No*

If no, enter the date the statement of absence was sent to the employee _____

When does the employee expect to return to work (enter the date) _____

Tear off along dotted line Supervisor's signature _____

- -

STATEMENT OF ABSENCE
EMPLOYEE'S DETAILS

Surname _____ Initials _____

Man No. _____ Branch/Dept. _____ Branch No. _____

TO BE COMPLETED BY EMPLOYEE

LENGTH OF ABSENCE

If known state the number of working days absent during period of absence _____

The date and time absence from work commenced _____

The date and time sickness or injury (if appropriate) commenced if not a working day _____

If known, state the date and time of return to employment _____

REASON FOR ABSENCE – If sickness or injury give details of symptoms and their development. Give any supporting evidence (e.g. diagnosis, treatment, witnesses, etc.)

_____

_____

_____

Have you visited a doctor?   Yes/No*   What was the date of visit? _____

I consent to the doctor being approached to verify my statement. His/her name and address or telephone no. is

I confirm that the above statement is true and acknowledge that any false statement may result in both my summary dismissal and/or criminal prosecution, as part of sickness benefit is of a statutory nature. (This statement will be retained in the Company records for a period of 3 years and may be shown to a Company medical adviser and D.H.S.S. officials)

Employee's signature _____   Date_____

NOT TO BE COMPLETED BY EMPLOYEE

I confirm that the above employee has been interviewed in respect of the above statement.

Supervisor/Management signature_____   Date_____

Has or will payment be authorized on appropriate wage amendment form?_____

Yes/No*   Manager's signature_____

*Delete as appropriate
N.B. THE NECESSARY DOCUMENTATION FOR WAGE AMENDMENT MUST BE COMPLETED.

Appendix 8
Managing a Job and a Family

Millions of workpeople have at least two jobs: the one they get paid for and the one they do at home. Frequently, mothers find that pressures at home have a profound effect on their ability to turn up for work.

Children who go to school catch childish illnesses. Epidemics don't discriminate. Childminders leave – and sometimes fail to turn up. Husbands/partners invariably believe *their* job is more important, and these influences invariably conspire to undermine commitment to work.

As one mother said: 'It's hard enough anyhow to bring up three kids, without having to cope with a job as well.' What are managers supposed to do about the problem? This simple checklist sets out some practical steps which can be taken:

1. Know which members of your team have families with dependent children (and, for that matter, sick or elderly relatives)
2. Monitor timekeeping carefully. She or he who has problems in getting to work on time is also likely to have problems with attendance. Sometimes lateness is an opportunity to talk with an individual
3. Be sympathetic to those with genuine difficulties. Try to meet them half-way on hours – either at the beginning or the end of the day
4. Talk to your personnel department about the possibility of 'during term only' contracts of employment
5. Look at opportunities for job re-design or internal transfers which may give some individuals more flexibility

6. *Let female employees talk to somebody female! Mothers understand other mothers. You can't expect to come to terms with emotional/parental/family issues, unless there's some common meeting point*

7. Be sensitive to the problems you encounter – don't be gung-ho or 'macho'. The last thing your employee needs is to be told she should have thought of all this before she accepted the job. Listen to what she has to say and think about it before you react. If you're a man with a wife or partner, ask her what she would do

8. Find out how other mothers cope with the problem and see if you can't cross-fertilize a few ideas

9. Insist on the individual taking some responsibility as well. You're there to help her solve her problems – not to manage them all for her

10. Don't give the game away by silly – or 'over-soft' – solutions. For example, if someone fails to turn up on Tuesday because one of the children is said to be unwell, don't let them make up the income they've lost by automatically doling out some overtime on Thursday. Use some common sense and make up your mind by *investigation* about the genuine needs involved

11. And, finally, remember one thing. Women with children go to work because they need the money. They may – or may not – also want careers or fulfilment. But they do need to supplement their partner's income – and sometimes there isn't a partner. If they don't turn up, it should not be assumed that they're lazy. At the same time, if communications between you aren't very good, all you'll get is a sick note (if that) and you'll never find out the cause of the problem.

Appendix 9
Sources of Help and Advice

1. Sargent-Minton Ltd: management consultants specializing in employee-relations techniques, training and consultancy; relevant subjects include motivation, communication, management development and training (telephone: 0702-471381)
2. Gillian Howard Associates: specialists in Industrial Relations Law who can provide advice on its interpretation (telephone: 01-435 3229)
3. Aikin, Ballentyne Partners (telephone: 01-727 9791)
4. Institute of Personnel Management (telephone: 01-946 9100)
5. Institute of Directors (telephone: 01-839 1233)
6. Incomes Data Services (telephone: 01-250 3434)
7. Industrial Society (telephone: 01-839 4300)